Goal-Driven
Management

Goal-Driven Management

Getting Back to the Basics

Glenn H. Varney, Ph.D.
Bowling Green State University

Lexington Books
D.C. Heath and Company/Lexington, Massachusetts/Toronto

89399

Library of Congress Cataloging-in-Publication Data

Varney, Glenn H.
  Goal-driven management

  Bibliography: p.
  Includes index.
  1. Management   I. Title.
HD31.V38   1986   658.4   86-45300
ISBN 0-669-13213-6 (alk. paper)

Published simultaneously in Canada
Printed in the United States of America
Casebound International Standard Book Number: 0-669-13213-6
Library of Congress Catalog Card Number: 86-45300

The paper used in this publication meets the minimum requirements of American National Standard for Information Sciences—Permanence of Paper for Printed Library Materials, ANSI Z39.48-1984. ∞™

86 87 88 89 90 8 7 6 5 4 3 2 1

Contents

Figures and Tables

Figures

Tables

Preface

Today's American managers are swamped with suggestions of how to improve their management skills. They are being given an ultimatum: catch up or lose out to competition. For many it is like being told they have been doing it wrong all these years.

American managers are the best in the world, and our foreign competitors have learned most of what they know about managing from U.S. organizations. How is it, then, that we seem to be falling behind? Is it our high cost of labor or the strong dollar? Or is it possible that we have strayed from the basics of management that were practiced so conscientiously in the past? A multitude of highly successful American companies are meeting the competition: Motorola, ITT, and General Electric, for example, have held their own, toe-to-toe, with the best the world has to offer.

There is a reason why some American companies are failing while others are succeeding: the winners believe in, and apply, some fundamental practices in management. They live by the basics, just as the winning football team practices and then follows the basics on the field.

To most managers, the basics are not new. "Of course I know the basics," they will say. But you must then ask: "Do you understand and practice them?" In the reality of the work setting, the answer is often, "No."

The basics are simply ideas that, when practiced, generate the forces that move our organizations ahead and keep them there. This book defines the core of these basics in terms that managers can understand and apply. For some, this book will serve as a reminder or refresher; for others, it will stimulate learning and change.

The following list presents a sample of the most important basics of management that have served to power American organizations.

Goal-driven organizations and individuals produce the highest achievements.

Goal-driven management, coupled with participative management, improves productivity within organizations.

Self-measurement of goal achievement stimulates high performance.

An investment in helping people yields improvement in individual and organizational performance.

Application of American productivity techniques yields performance improvements.

Teaching and helping people to apply cost-containment concepts keeps an organization functioning on a "lean and hungry" basis.

Planning beyond one year, at all levels in the organization, alerts the entire organization to changes in the environment.

Practicing established and tested organizational-change approaches assures the flexibility in organizations necessary to meet the competition.

Developing work-team management skills uses the combined talents of all individuals, resulting in higher productivity and quality.

Designing a system to stimulate and monitor the organization assures that it will not be caught "napping."

Learning from each other, especially from other American companies, stimulates change and creativity in our organizations.

This book provides a brief, to-the-point analysis of these basics. To test your level of understanding, a brief quiz is supplied at the end of each chapter. You will find these self-examinations useful and easy to complete. Simply respond to each question with a yes or no answer. It may not be a simple choice, but we encourage you to take a position one way or another. If you respond no to a question, make a few notations in the space provided, and these notations should help to clarify why you responded the way that you did.

After you complete each quiz, count the negative responses. The more negative responses, the more you need to learn about that particular area of goal-driven management.

1
American Goal-Driven Management: A Cycle of Improvement

> Love our principle, order our foundation, progress our goal.
> —Auguste Comte

Within the hardship setting of World War II, MIT's Dr. Kurt Lewin studied the buying habits of housewives. He found that wartime housewives displayed an apparently natural ability to determine how far their limited funds and rationing stamps could be stretched. Then they established purchasing plans according to their immediate household needs and resources. This type of goal-setting activity, Lewin pointed out, has never been limited to wartime or to housewives; goal setting plays a significant role in almost everyone's day-to-day existence. From this idea, the general character of goal-driven management was formed.

In its simplest design, goal-driven management is deciding what goal an individual wants to reach, finding ways to attain the desired goal, and establishing standards to measure whether or not the goal has been reached. The key factor is recognizing that a goal must be keyed to the individual's sense of what needs to be done and that as a result, a highly personalized approach to setting goals should evolve.

Three Essential Notions for Effective Use of Goal-Driven Management

1. A manager must understand the behavioral implications of goal-driven management, specifically why it can become an important motivator. People perform most effectively when their needs are met within the workplace, and a manager must recognize and respond to these needs.

   a. People need to know how they are expected to function in their particular job.

   b. On the job, a sense of participation and self-direction is important to people.

   c. People need to receive feedback on how well a particular job is performed.

d. From time to time, people need the manager's advice and guidance to accomplish their desired goals.

e. People feel a sense of satisfaction and accomplishment from doing a job well, and they need to receive recognition for that well done job.

2. Traditionally, managers have functioned in an authoritarian manner. The authoritarian manager makes *every* decision, from setting goals for the organization, to assigning individual jobs, to dictating specific procedures. The individual is relegated to following the authoritarian manager's orders, or else!

When a manager decides to use goal-driven management, the authoritarian style of management no longer applies. Managers must appeal to employees' personal drive, and recognize that authoritarian behavior thwarts the ambition of others. Often, a manager must change his/her style of leadership, which can be quite difficult for someone accustomed to making all decisions. With goal-driven management, many decisions a manager used to make alone must now be shared with various individuals. If decision-making is shared, individuals are more involved in the organization's activities, come to understand much more about the job, feel more autonomous, and require less monitoring.

3. When a manager attempts to implement goal-driven management, the skills of perception and communication must be developed to a high level. Such skills include:

a. The ability to listen
b. The art of asking open-minded, probing questions
c. The ability to diagnose, investigate, and evaluate work-performance and the variables affecting work
d. The ability to give accurate advice and guidance

The Performance-Improvement Cycle

A close examination of events over a period of time reveals that most function in a cycle; that is, events proceed through a series of logical steps to a conclusion, and then the steps are repeated.

Goal-driven management works as a cycle within an organization. In fact, thinking about performance as a series of logical steps helps to clarify the functions of management and helps a manager to understand the dynamics of the process as it applies to his/her job.

*The Time Dimensions of the Performance-Improvement
Cycle*

Because we are dealing with time as the main variable in an improvement cycle (the very nature of any cycle necessitates that a certain span of time must pass, during which the cycle may be completed—a cycle cannot be completed instantaneously), it is important to have some sense of the length and scope of the cycle. In a traditional business organization, the financial cycle is completed at least once a year, at which time a report is rendered to the stockholders and to officials of the organization. There are some companies that find it beneficial to complete the financial cycle more frequently, establishing monthly, weekly, or even daily cycles. Due to the obvious connections between performance and financial results, the performance-improvement cycle is frequently subservient to the financial cycle.

However, the peformance-improvement cycle should not be governed solely by the financial cycle. The performance-improvement cycle should maintain a time span of twelve months, and it should never be extended beyond this period except under unusual circumstances. Customarily, the time span is shorter: once a month, or at a minimum, quarterly. The frequency of the peformance-improvement cycle is largely determined by the nature of the individual business, and commonly it will vary from one department to the next. In a research department, since progress-review meetings are usually held monthly and/or bimonthly, it is desirable to establish the performance-improvement cycle on a matching schedule.

In situations where the time factor is critical, it is often desirable to shorten the cycle to match the urgency of the particular situation. A list of the critical factors that need to be studied before determining the length of the cycle include:

1. *The urgency of the situation.* Under tight financial conditions and close scheduling, a shorter cycle is more advantageous.

2. *Existing control systems within the organization.* For example, production-reporting systems that report on a biweekly basis might be one of the factors determining how frequently the cycle should be completed.

3. *How eager a manager is to master goal-driven management.* The shorter the cycle—and, therefore the more frequently a cycle is completed—the faster a person learns how to be a goal-driven manager.

4. *The speed with which an undesirable variation can occur, and the magnitude of the consequences of such a problem.* For example, in space technology a very simple error can cost millions of dollars. If such errors could be corrected immediately, through a shorter cycle, the loss could perhaps be avoided, or at least minimized.

There are numerous advantages to shorter cycles, not the least of which is the more accurate control the employee gains over his/her work.

Elements of the Performance-Improvement Cycle

There are four main elements to the cycle, and they flow in the following order:

Define the job

Design goals

Execute the task

Measure results

The flow of this cycle is shown graphically in figure 1–1.

It is imperative to understand that peformance-improvement cycles are interlocked within a larger series of cycles that cover a significant (that is several years) span of time. Each successive performance-improvement cycle is a segment in an upward progression, as figure 1–2 illustrates.

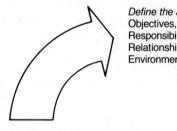

Define the Job
Objectives,
Responsibilities,
Relationships, and
Environment

Measure Results
Difference between
Expected vs. Actual
Design Correction Plans

Design Goals
Quantitative
Qualitative
Rewards

Execute Task
Qualified
Trained
Motivated

Figure 1–1. Individual Performance-Improvement Cycle

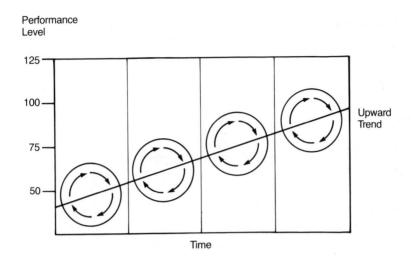

Figure 1–2. A Series of Individual Performance-Improvement Cycles

Define the Job. A job is defined by the key responsibilities for which an employee is held accountable. These key responsibilities normally describe eighty to ninety percent of what the employee actually does, and they are defined in terms broad enough to provide the employee with a healthy degree of freedom.

In any job, each key responsibility is assigned a value of relative importance. Managers should assess relative importance in terms of the employee's *time input,* or how much time must be expended to achieve the desired result(s). An employee might have four key responsibilities, but it is quite possible that sixty to seventy percent of the employee's time is spent on the two most important responsibilities. Each key responsibility must be ranked on a scale of relative importance.

Characteristically, the functions that a manager/employee performs can be clustered into groups of similar activities and duties. For the purpose of illustration, we have provided a sample worksheet, in which a personnel administrator has defined the key responsibilities of his/her job (see table 1–1).

To identify and define key job responsibilities, first list all of the duties and actions that are part of your job (column A). Second, take these various duties and actions and group them into related clusters (column B). The third and final step is to establish a set of word descriptions to define the clusters of related duties and actions that you listed in column B (column C).

When establishing such descriptions, don't provide specific details, but define the broader scope of the key job responsibilities. Such descriptions should be confined to approximately five to ten words, should not be pro-

Table 1–1
Key Job Responsibility Worksheet, page 1

A. Duties and Actions of Your Job	B. Grouping of Related Duties and Actions	C. Key Job Responsibilities	R I

1. Recruit and assist in hiring clerical, professional (college recruiting) and managerial personnel for the company.	1. 1 Recruit and assist in hiring
	        Clerical
	        College
	        Management
	        personnel.
	   10 Aid to education program.
		1. Manage manpower-recruitment (internal and external) program.	20

2. Design and conduct training and management-development programs.			
3. Manage the manpower recruiting and development department of 15 people.	2. 2 Design and conduct training. 4 Administer college-trainee program.	2. Manage manpower and management-development program.	20
4. Administer college-trainee programs.	3. 3 Supervise recruiting and manpower-development staff. 5 Budget and control expenses.	3. Supervise, plan, organize and maintain an effective department.	40
5. Plan budget for department and control expenses.			
6. Assist in management of personnel department.	4. 6 Assist in management of personnel department. 8 Consult and assist department heads.	4. Provide assistance and consultive service.	20
7. Research and keep abreast of changes in the field.			
8. Consult with department heads on recruiting and manpower-development matters.	5. 7 Research and keep abreast. 9 Maintain salaried records.	5.	
9. Maintain all salaried-personnel records.	6.	6.	
10. Assist in planning and administration of aid to education/contribution programs.			

Source: Dr. Glenn H. Varney, Management By Objectives. Chicago, Ill.: The Dartnell Co., p. 84. Reprinted with permission.

cedural in nature, and should describe only the basic, key responsibilities for which the manager/employee is held accountable.

Design Goals. For any key responsibility, there exists a goal. A goal can be expressed by:

1. Quantity of product/service
2. Quality of product/service
3. Value (monetary) of product/service
4. Punctuality of performance

Each goal has a relative importance value that corresponds to the relative importance of the specific key responsibility to which it is linked.

Although it is not uncommon for a key responsibility to have more than one goal, it is important for a manager to sort out and focus upon the goals most essential and crucial to the key responsibility at hand. In so doing, a manager can isolate those critical components which best reveal whether or not the job as a whole is successfully performed.

There are two general rules that are useful when designing and setting goals.

1. Each key responsibility should have no more than three goals. It is advisable to start out with a small number of clearly defined goals, and then, if necessary, add to these as you move ahead.
2. Goals must meet a set of criteria to determine the quality and feasibility of their design.

The first step in designing goals is to transfer the list of key responsibilities to column C on the second page of the worksheet (see table 1–2). (For brevity's sake, only two of the personnel administrator's key responsibilities are provided.) The second step is to obtain present performance-measurement data, to be used as an aid in designing goals (the data is not listed). The third step is to actually design the goals for each key responsibility, remembering that goals are to be expressed in terms of quantity, quality, value, and punctuality (column D). The final step in designing and setting goals is testing them to determine if they meet the criteria of a well-designed goal. The criteria follow.

1. Can the individual responsible for the job control all aspects of the job that affect the goal, and does the goal represent a major segment of the individual's responsibility?
2. Can the individual reach the goal, and will he/she have to stretch a bit to do so? A goal must not be set so high that it is unobtainable.
3. Does the goal relate directly to the goals for the individual's boss, for the department, and for the organization as a whole?
4. Can the goal be exceeded, and can the individual fall below the goal if he/she fails to perform on the job? An individual should be able to excel on the job.
5. Is there a way to provide direct feedback to the individual about his/her progress towards the goal?
6. Can achievement towards the goal be clearly measured at the end of one performance-improvement cycle?

Table 1–2
Key Job Responsibility Worksheet, page 2

C. Key Job Responsibilities	D. Goals			E. Expected Results Tests	
1. Management/ Manpower Recruitment Programs a. College b. Internal promotion, transfer c. Clerical and professional, outside	1. College Clerical Professional	Accept ratio 40% 50% 65%	Cost/man hired $775 150 1050	1 2 3 4 5 6	X X X X X X
	2. College Clerical Professional	Percent goal filled 95% — 85%	Time to fill (in days) — 14 days 40 days	1 2 3 4 5 6	X X X X X X
	3. Two new, creative ideas each, to improve effectiveness of college recruiting, clerical and professional recruitment: Criteria (1) Recognized by outside company as new innovations, (2) Actual results (comments, number hired etc.) of innovation.			1 2 3 4 5 6	X X X X X X
2. Supervise, plan, organize, and maintain an effective department.	1. A. Prepare an annual budget and have approved on schedule. Include 10% cost reduction in one phase of operation equal to $10,000 annual savings. B. Stay within budget limits, +5% and −10%.			1 2 3 4 5 6	X X X X X X
	2. A. Maintain a 95-level-attitude index for members of staff. B. Hold quarterly "deep sensing" meeting and report findings and action steps within 10 days. C. Maintain turnover at: Promotion: 1 person per year Termination: 5% per year			1 2 3 4 5 6	
	3.			1 2 3 4 5 6	

Source: Dr. Glenn A. Varney, Management By Objectives. Chicago, Ill.: The Dartnell Co., p. 85. Reprinted with permission.

In column D, you will find that the personnel administrator's goals have been tested against each of the criteria, and an *X* indicates that the goals have passed the tests. The second goal of key responsibility number two has been left blank so that you may test it to determine whether or not it is well designed.

Executing the Task. Obviously, the individual on the job is the most critical cog in the performance-improvement cycle. It is the individual who assumes the key responsibilities, who is expected to achieve the goals, who executes the task, and whose performance is measured. The competency of the individual within the context of the job is what gets the job done; and it is this competency that the performance-improvement cycle is designed to improve.

Measure Results. To complete the performance-improvement cycle, actual results are compared with goals; this is the most sensitive phase in the cycle. It is important to think of goal-driven management as a series of logical steps that are subject to rational and tangible measurement and a high degree of objective control.

Given a well-designed job and a competent employee, we can reasonably expect that the goals and results, which are compatible with the employee and the job, will be achieved. In other words, results should live up to goals. This, however, is not always the case.

Generally speaking, the focus in the past has been on the individual, rather than the key responsibilities and goals that the individual is working towards. In the goal-driven management approach, the focus is first of all upon the results the individual produces, secondly upon the key responsibilities the individual is accountable for, and thirdly upon the individual's competency in performing the job. Therefore, we begin to move away from the highly personal, sometimes overly critical, appraisal systems that have concentrated upon the individual's failure or success.

The following presents the steps that are involved in the performance-measuring phase:

1. Establish the level of performance.
2. Explore reasons why the level is where it is.
3. Decide upon plans for correcting or expanding performance.

This phase is conducted during a face-to-face meeting, and each of these steps is a distinct entity.

When establishing the level of performance, actual results are measured against goals. It is essential for managers to examine fully the overall scheme before tackling individual segments of performance. Corrective plans may go awry if one element of the job or goal is adjusted without regard to the broader context.

The second step is to explore, diagnose, and evaluate the reasons for the existence of variations above or below the actual goals that had previously been set. In seeking the answers, you and the individual should examine all the job elements that may contribute to the problem. Next, look over goals to see if there are possible explanations to be found in this area. You should determine if the goals have been set too high and are perhaps unattainable.

The final step is to design corrective plans on the basis of the diagnosis. This may involve changing the job design or the job structure. You may need to design developmental and training programs in the areas where individuals need help.

When looking at the performance-measuring phase, four basic rules should be followed.

1. Take one step at a time. First, decide how the individual is performing and at what level. Second, diagnose and evaluate the results in terms of the job, the goals, and the individual. And third, design plans for solving the problems and raising the individual's level of performance.

2. Look at all three steps as an integral part of the performance-improvement session and consider this the pivotal meeting in the goal-driven management program.

3. Look at each goal individually, carefully setting them so that the worker is able and motivated to attain them.*

4. Finally, look at the balance between one goal and another, and one part of the job and another, to understand the relationship between each expected total effect. This means that when something is adjusted in one part of the job or one goal, it is quite reasonable to expect that there will be some effect that shows up in some other part of the job or in some other goal. Therefore, when an adjustment is made, a manager should carefully look at each aspect of the job and the goals that the individual is working towards to ascertain the effect from that adjustment. This extremely important consideration is frequently overlooked by the manager.

When Goal-Driven Management Fails to Work

If a manager's approach is hasty or haphazard, certain pitfalls of which the manager is not aware may be unavoidable. Some of these traps are discussed below.

---

*The specific process of goal-setting is often mistaken as the whole point of goal-driven management, but goal-driven management is much more than merely setting goals. Goals are easy to set. The value of goal-driven management is that it helps an individual to set the *right* goal and to *reach* those goals.

1. If you concentrate too much on the abstract workings of the system, and fail to develop a personal interaction with the employees that the system is designed to help, the outcome will be a frustrated manager. It *is* important to understand the system, but it is just as important to communicate this understanding to other people; the success in making goal-driven management work depends on your ability to teach the system.

2. If people think of the system as an added responsibility, they will view it as simply more work. They may even feel that they have been told to do someone else's work. You must emphasize that goal-driven management is not added work but an opportunity for people to manage their own activities.

3. If your staff hasn't had much experience managing its own activities, then you will have to help the staff develop the necessary skills. Before you can expect goal-driven management to work, you must consider how extreme the behavioral changes are that you expect your people to make.

4. If you ask your employees to change their behavior but you don't change yours, the result will be conflict since you aren't following your own advice.

5. Sometimes a manager will inadvertently control the goal-setting process. If you perform the goal-setting process for someone else, you cannot realistically expect him/her to follow it through.

6. If you're after a quick fix, forget it. Because goal-driven management requires many people to change their behavior, it cannot create an "overnight success." It may take as long as ten years to install effectively goal-driven management throughout an entire organization.

Four Keys to Success

1. A manager's basic beliefs about how people should function in an organization will affect his/her ability to use goal-driven management. If a manager believes that people need to be led, dictated to, or told exactly how to function, then goal-driven management will probably not work. On the other hand, if a manager believes that people have the competence, ability, and willingness to accept the responsibility to control their own work activities, then goal-driven management will probably work.

2. A manager must be willing to learn all the behavioral implications of goal-driven management and develop a clear understanding of how and by what means people are motivated.

3. The importance of interpersonal communication skills cannot be stressed enough. A manager must always be striving to further develop his/her skills of listening, questioning, communicating, and diagnosing.

4. No attempt should be made to immediately implement goal-driven management on a broad basis. To successfully use goal-driven management, a manager needs a systematic understanding of how it works, combined with

an ability to teach it, and a step-by-step plan to implement the program. Starting with the development of a manager's own ability to become goal-driven, goal-driven management should extend slowly, individual by individual, unit by unit, throughout the entire organization. Goal-driven management is a system of management that will work *only* if the manager takes the time to carefully design, implement, test, and diagnose each of the basic steps while maintaining an openness and a willingness to trust others and share responsibility.

2
Goal-Driven Management and Theory Z: The Emerging Style

Progress, therefore, is not an accident, but a necessity—it is a part of nature.
—Herbert Spencer

Research and practical experience have demonstrated that certain human qualities produce positive results within organizations. The most significant of these qualities is the human desire to achieve, and this intense desire is the cornerstone of goal-driven management.

Dr. David McClelland at Harvard University has identified a number of conditions that an organization needs to maximize to arouse the achievement drive in individuals.

The Achievement Drive Is Aroused When:

1. Specific goals of the job are made explicit.
2. Goals represent a moderate degree of risk for the individual involved.
3. Goals can be adjusted as the situation warrants, especially when they vary widely from a fifty-fifty chance of accomplishment.
4. Individuals receive feedback after successfully reaching their goals.
5. Individual responsibility for the successful outcome is stressed.
6. Rewards, and lack thereof, within the control system in which the individual operates are perceived as consistent with achievement of goals.
7. There is a climate of mutual support, encouragement, and understanding.

The object of any management system, when considering the human aspects of the organization, should be to maximize (1) the degree to which people are involved in the process of making the system work, (2) the degree to which they are allowed to function independently within the boundaries of the organization, and (3) the degree to which they are able to develop a sense of achievement. Both goal-driven management and theory Z aim to promote such managerial systems.

Theory Z was introduced by Dr. William Ouchi to compare and contrast various styles of managing.[1] Simply put, it is a description of the most successful companies in America. In his book entitled *Theory Z,* Dr. Ouchi declares that there are two basic types of American organizations: the *traditional* American organization (Type A), and the *alternative* American organization (Type Z). The distinguishing features of each type are compared here.

Type A *Traditional Organization*	*Type Z* *Alternative Organization*
Short-term employment	Long-term employment
Individual decision-making	Consensual decision-making
Individual responsibility	Individual responsibility
Rapid evaluation/promotion	Slow evaluation/promotion
Explicit, formalized controls	Implicit, informal controls (with explicit, formalized goals)
Specialized career paths	Generalized career paths
Segmented concern for person	Holistic concern for person

The type A organization is top-heavy; almost all planning and control functions are performed by top management, with relatively little input from lower levels of the organization. The highest management level dictates to the rest of the organization. In the past, this system proved profitable enough; but now individuals want their own voices to be heard.

Individuals' voices are heard in a type Z organization. Because they are aware that the individual's role is of central importance, these organizations exhibit a unique consideration for the individual. There is a high level of concern for, and recognition of, the needs of employees within the organizational structure. In a type Z organization, each individual is involved in, and responsible for, at least some portion of the planning and controlling functions of management; top-heaviness is discarded in favor of balance. The result is a more productive, motivated, and dedicated workforce.

Goal-driven management seeks to achieve exactly this result. Accordingly, if management provides for the basic needs of the individuals asked to achieve organizational goals, then the individuals will, in return, feel significantly more involved in the organization and strive harder to achieve said goals.

In essence, goal-driven management seeks to convert type A organizations into type Z organizations, and in fact, many of the organizations that Dr. Ouchi cites as type Z examples have already been practicing some form of goal-driven management. Type Z companies serve as models for the emerging style of management, one that is necessary to meet today's challenges and tomorrow's potential nightmares. Goal-driven management serves as the mechanism for continued survival and growth.

Today, we do have robots in the workplace, robots that do exactly as they are told without saying a word, robots made of circuits and steel. The flesh and blood of our workforce is not content to be treated as robots, nor are they likely to continue to work silently. Our employees have voices, desires, ideas, and opinions. Type Z organizations are tapping this invaluable resource, and goal-driven-management is the right tool to bring it forth.

New Aggregate of Management Skills

To be an effective manager under either a theory Z or goal-driven-management approach, the following skills are required:

Negotiation	Intrinsic motivation
Career-counseling	Problem-solving
Collaboration	Group dynamics
Delegation	Conflict-resolution

These skills are not new in the management literature, but often they are considered singularly. For instance, it is not uncommon to teach negotiation skills to managers, but it is very uncommon to find management-development programs in which *all* of these basic management skills are taught. To be an effective manager in the future, one must be able to perform effectively all of the skills listed above.

Practical Questions

When managers examine goal-driven management or theory Z management systems, they usually ask questions about the application of either concept to an established organizational context. Some of these questions are easily answered, others are not. The typical questions raised include some of the following.

1. *How do you get a traditional American company to change?* Obviously, any company that has been deeply steeped in traditional American management is not likely to change overnight. Frequently, something just short of a revolution is required.

2. *What is likely to happen if a company or organization refuses to change?* Ever hear of the dinosaurs?

3. *Do goal-driven management and theory Z apply to government and other forms of organizations?* Anywhere that you find human beings working together within organizations, you will find that these concepts are appropriate. Within some organizations, such a change is more appropriate and easier to install than in others.

4. Are there organizations that can still get by using the traditional American approach? The answer is yes, of course! There are organizations in this country primarily made up of older employees with very traditional approaches to managing, and in such organizations the traditional system is still quite appropriate.

But even in these more traditional organizations you will find that the traditional approach is not working as well as it used to work. It is generally agreed that if it does not make a major change in its organizational management, General Motors will not be successful in the future. GM recognizes this, which is the reason for its thrust into the "Quality of Work Life" (QWL) program now underway.

5. If you can get management to agree to the change, how would you proceed? There is no simple answer to this question, as one might expect. The best approach is to understand what other organizations have done, to be aware of the experiences they have had, to know what the literature has to say about organizations, and to develop a unique plan for the organization that is attempting to change. Design the change process to fit that particular organization's needs and proceed accordingly.

The change will not be easy. Any time an organization attempts to move from the form of management in which it is deeply entrenched to another, the change process is slow and painful.

Note

1. William Ouchi, *Theory Z* (Addison-Wesley, 1981).

Quiz

Goal-Driven Management and Theory Z: The Emerging Style

1. Are you applying theory Z concepts to your
    organization?

    _____   _____
    Yes   No

2. Does your goal-setting process provide autonomy
    and freedom for your employees?

    _____   _____
    Yes   No

3. Do you have *all* of the needed skills to manage a
   theory Z organization?

              Yes   No

3
Individual Behavior and Goal Achievement

Change the environment; do not try to change man.
—Richard Buckminster Fuller

Performance appraisal has long been a concern of management, and it continues to be so today. Some reasons for the use of performance appraisal systems include: improvement of performance, EEOC documentation, compensation justification, developmental purposes, and union documentation. These reasons alone are enough to clearly justify the development of a workable performance appraisal system.

The types of systems which have been developed over the years include: merit-rating systems, critical-incident systems, rank-order systems, standards of performance, goals systems, peer-review systems, assessment-center approaches, individual-employee contracting (as with a subcontractor), third-party evaluation, and recently, retranslation of expectations. At this time, no system is flawless; there are both strengths and weaknesses in all of these systems.

A recent development in performance appraisal is the system of behaviorally anchored rating scales (BARS). The idea behind this approach was to develop a more methodical and valid system of evaluating performance—a system that would not only stand up in court in case of EEOC complaints, but would also help individuals evaluate their own performance.

Unfortunately, there is no single system that can accomplish all objectives, and any system is only as good as the people who use it. Thus, there is no perfect system.

Criteria for Effective Appraisal Systems

Before examining the BARS approach in conjunction with the goal-setting process, examine some of the criteria used to decide if a performance-appraisal system is effective:

1. Is the performance-appraisal system accepted by employees?
2. Is it fair and equable in dealing with differences between employees?
3. Is it clearly understood by both those using it and those affected by it?

4. Is it based on the individual's work performance or on personal characteristics?
5. Does it provide useful data for the employee, as well as the supervisor?
6. Does it react to changes in the job and the employee's work environment?

All of these criteria need to be considered, and an attempt should be made to meet them as new systems of performance appraisal are developed. BARS comes very close to meeting these criteria.

The prerequisites for a successful system of performance appraisal include:

1. A well-defined and accurately communicated set of goals
2. A concrete and mutually agreed upon set of behaviors required to reach the goals
3. The effective interaction between employee and supervisor

A Concept of Performance Improvement

As one thinks about the way in which work is accomplished within an organization, three obvious factors emerge:

Resources   A person must have the finances, equipment, and staff required to get the job done.

Goals   A person must have a clearly defined and measurable set of goals.

Behavior   Not only must the required resources be available to the employee, but the employee must make proper use of these resources.

This interaction is portrayed in figure 3–1.

What is BARS (Behaviorally Anchored Rating Scales)?

BARS is used to define what behaviors are required to make proper use of the available resources to achieve a goal. In its simplest form, BARS is nothing more than the establishment of specific statements which describe below-average, adequate, and clearly superior behavior. Such statements can then be scaled from one to nine, as illustrated in figure 3–2.

The objective of developing BARS is to establish scales for each of the key goals that towards which a person is working. It is possible to have as many as two or three scales for each goal, as several different behaviors may

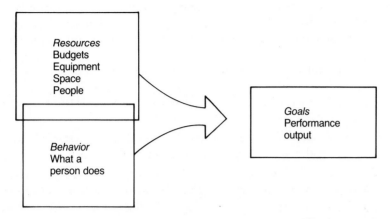

Figure 3–1. Relationship of Goals, Behavior, and Resources

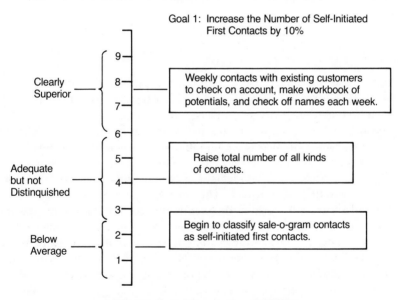

Figure 3–2. Example of BARS

be associated with achievement of a specific goal. Sometimes one behavior is related to more than one goal, so the same scaling could be applied to each goal.

In general, behaviors must be described in specific terms. They need to be observable, so that they can be measured while being performed. When behaviors have been completed, they should be precisely evaluated. It is essential that behaviors have been mutually agreed upon in advance, so that the employee understands exactly what is expected. What is most important is that there should be no question about which behaviors are acceptable and which are not.

There are still some difficulties related to the problem of using BARS.

1. Many different behaviors (often ones that are difficult to observe) may affect results.

2. We tend to remember only those behaviors that are extremely good or extremely bad, while losing track of the in-between ones.

3. We sometimes allow our preexisting opinions of a person to color or distort our perceptions of that person's behavior, selectively remembering those behaviors that confirm our opinions, forgetting those that disagree with our opinions.

4. In a goal-oriented program, goals are easiest to discuss. Thus, the tendency is to talk about goals and goal-achievement, at the expense of behaviors.

Diagnosis of Ineffective Performance

The aim of such diagnosis is to pinpoint the problem behavior. Once the ineffective behavior has been located and isolated, the exact nature of the problem becomes much clearer and easier to correct.

As an example, let's look at a teacher whose performance is evaluated by his students. This is his first teaching job, and he has held it for three years. He talks a lot and is strong-willed. His goal is to maintain or exceed a rating of 2.8, a rating based on his students' satisfaction with his performance. But, he receives a rating of only 2.3. The obvious question is, "Why did this teacher fall short of his goal?" By examining two behaviors—his teaching style and his willingness to help students—the answer to this question becomes clear. The variables of the evaluation can be plotted on a two-by-two matrix (see figure 3–3). Since the result fell below the goal, this will be indicated as Low on both matrices. On the other hand, one of his behaviors (his willingness to help students) was excellent, while the other (his teaching style) was deficient. The excellent behavior will show up as High on one matrix, and the deficient behavior will show up as Low on the other matrix. The Low/Low box clearly shows which behavior is adversely influencing results.

A matrix can be established to examine any set of observable behaviors and results, and the rudimentary setup is shown in figure 3–4.

A matrix provides a simple illustration that identifies the problem area (we all know how many words a picture is worth). Each box in figure 3–5 proposes a different set of considerations and questions to be evaluated during the performance-appraisal interview.

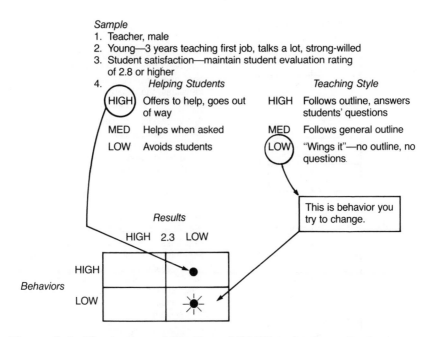

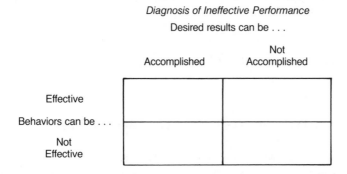

Figure 3–3. Illustration of the Use of BARS to Improve Performance

Figure 3–4. Matrix for Study of Performance Related to Behaviors and Results

The use of BARS in conjunction with the goal-setting process provides the employee with a clearly defined set of goals and a set of behaviors necessary to effectively achieve those goals. This clarity establishes a greater understanding of job requirements, and the appraisal interview is more productive with the visual aid of the matrices. A considerable amount of time is needed to establish the BARS system in conjunction with goal-setting, but

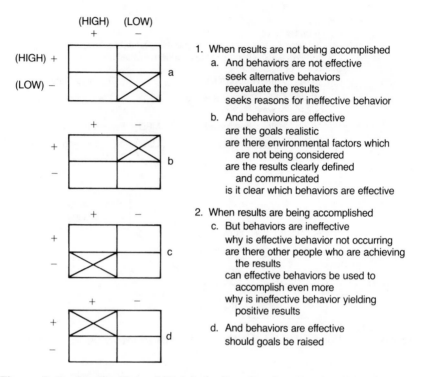

1. When results are not being accomplished
   a. And behaviors are not effective
      seek alternative behaviors
      reevaluate the results
      seeks reasons for ineffective behavior

   b. And behaviors are effective
      are the goals realistic
      are there environmental factors which
         are not being considered
      are the results clearly defined
         and communicated
      is it clear which behaviors are effective

2. When results are being accomplished
   c. But behaviors are ineffective
      why is effective behavior not occurring
      are there other people who are achieving
         the results
      can effective behaviors be used to
         accomplish even more
      why is ineffective behavior yielding
         positive results

   d. And behaviors are effective
      should goals be raised

Figure 3–5. Application of Matrix in Conducting the Appraisal Interview

this investment of time will be handsomely repaid, as the following testament shows.

Goal-Setting, Performance-Feedback, and Reinforcement

How Jacobsen Saved More Than $1,000,000 a Year

Howard McPherson is the general manager of the Turf Products Division for Jacobsen Manufacturing, a multimillion dollar company in the commercial and consumer grounds-maintenance business. One of the reports that Howard uses to make decisions is his quality performance report. This report gives a detailed monthly breakdown on the quality cost of doing business, including warranty, rejects, rework, scrap, and inspection cost. Over a six-month period, Howard's staff initiated a series of performance-improvement steps, including a behavioral analysis of key job activities, workshops for key employees, and implementation of performance-improvement projects. Over that same six-month period, the cost of quality to the company dropped significantly: savings were running in excess of a million dollars a year.

Three primary phases were undertaken at Jacobsen.

1. An *analytical phase* looked at the areas that needed improvement, examined desired performance levels, and clarified goals that were unclear or hazy. This required examining the actual performance of individuals in relation to the desired performance. Causes of any discrepancy between actual and desired performance levels were analyzed by using behavioral analysis techniques.

2. A *skill-building phase* was initiated for management and supervisory personnel, once the causes of the performance deficiency had been analyzed and converted into potential dollar returns. A two-day building workshop was conducted for key management personnel, and at later dates, one-day briefing sessions were held for supervisory employees.

3. As soon as the training sessions were completed, an *implementation phase* was scheduled during which solutions to performance discrepancies were initiated. Working with contacts within the company, outside consultants established target-performance levels, designed feedback systems that both met the needs of the accounting and operations departments, and made a strong psychological impact on employees, and coached managers and supervisors to use those feedback systems as a basis for reinforcement. Wherever possible, employees in the operating departments were directly involved in the change. This involvement pays off not only by bringing change about, but also be ensuring that implemented solutions are employed over an extended period of time.

One of the key changes at Jacobsen involved the quality-performance report. As a feedback mechanism, it met the needs of upper management by giving them an overall view of what was happening in quality-control. However, as an operating document and feedback mechanism, it was seriously deficient. There was no way, for example, for sections of the welding department to determine what their scrap was as a percentage of direct-labor dollars. So, one of the first steps taken was to change the information-gathering and feedback system used in this particular situation. Scrap and rework information was fed directly and quickly to the individual cost-center responsible for it. Although supervisors in charge of each cost-center had a general idea of their performance (that is, we are doing pretty well, we are doing okay, we are doing pretty poorly), they now had specific information about scrap and rework performance.

The changes in the feedback system, combined with the analytical work done earlier, resulted in an interesting phenomenon. Scrap appeared to almost double in the first month of the project. The reason for this was quite simple. The analysis showed that actual scrap was reported approximately twice as scrap. Previously, for every piece of scrap reported, another piece of scrap went unreported. This is a common occurrence in many organizations. What usually happens when an employee turns in a scrap piece is that he/she is "chewed" out and punished. The conversation usually goes something like this: "Mr. Supervisor, I'm afraid I've made a bad piece here, and I have to turn it in to be scrap." "You idiot, if I've told you once, I've told you a hundred times, we can't produce scrap here. Now get back to your machine and worker harder."

The result of this, of course, is that the employee learns that it doesn't pay to report scrap. The only thing that happens when you report scrap is that somebody gets angry. At Jacobsen, however, as a result of the skill-training workshop, supervisors were able to see how *proper* use of reinforcement techniques can be used, not only to get employees to report scrap accurately, but also, and more importantly, to get them to help get the scrap problem under control. After the skill-training, supervisors were more likely to be involved in a situation like this: "Mr. Supervisor, I'm afraid I have to report a scrap." "Mike, I appreciate your reporting the scrap. It's important to us to keep accurate records, so that we can know when we have to tackle a problem. However, as you may remember, we discussed this last week, and we are concerned about reducing the scrap. What do you think we could do to keep scrap down under one-half of one percent of direct-labor hours?"

When the employee replied with an appropriate answer, he would again be reinforced by the supervisor.

In the quality-performance report, feedback was provided, not only in the form of numbers, but also in the form of helpful graphs. If you walked through the various offices and shop areas at Jacobsen now, you would see a representative sample of graphs depicting total cost of quality as a percentage of direct-labor dollars, total scrap, scrap by department, rework by each department, total rework, and other information that people in operating positions use everyday to make decisions.

Another phase of implementing feedback and reinforcement systems involves purchasing-and-receiving personnel. As part of the implementation process to improve vendor performance, specific goals were established to allow receiving personnel to monitor their own performance (thus providing a basis for reinforcement by supervisor personnel). Also, a feedback system was set up from purchasing to receiving, to help receiving personnel translate their efforts into dollars for the company. Thus, on a regular basis, receiving-room personnel sent a list of checked shipments to purchasing, with a note stating where the shipments were short of, or beyond, prescribed limits; then, purchasing fed back to receiving-room personnel data on how much money they had saved the company that week by finding the short shipments. As the productivity of receiving went up in terms of shipments checked, these improvements were reinforced by various management and supervisory personnel.

While these are by no means all the steps implemented by this firm, they are representative of some of the different goals established, feedback systems installed, and reinforcements used. Savings have been well worth the efforts that went into the project. On an annualized basis, Jacobsen is realizing savings of more than $1,000,000 a year. Although management also feels that these efforts will have a long-term benefit in warranty and field-service costs, such benefits are not expected to show up for several more years. It is not possible to directly relate any projected changes to the efforts that went into this project. Other performance improvements that came about as a result of the implemented changes include fewer line delays (due to increased availability of quality parts), better working relationships between departments, and more aggressive problem-tackling by employees.

In short, when you ask Howard if combining goal-setting with feedback and reinforcement works, he answers with a million-dollar smile.

References: For further information on MBO and BARS, read these articles.

"Developing Behaviorally Anchored Rating Scales (BARS)," C. E. Schneider and R. W. Beatty, APD, *The Personnel Administrator,* August 1979.

"Combining BARS and MBO: Using an Appraisal System to Diagnose Performance Problems," C. R. Schneir and R. W. Beatty, APD, *The Personnel Administrator,* September 1979.

Quiz

Individual Behavior and Goal Achievement

1. Does your performance appraisal system work well?

                             Yes   No

   Comments:

2. Does your performance appraisal system tend to be subjective rather than objective, leading employees to question your judgment about performance appraisal?

                             Yes   No

   Comments:

3. Do you understand how the three elements of performance—resources, behaviors, and goals—interact to help an individual do a job effectively?

                             Yes   No

   Comments:

4. Have you been successful in getting employees to take responsibility for improving their own individual performance?

                             Yes   No

   Comments:

4
Helping People Improve

> Man can learn nothing unless he proceeds from the known to the unknown.
> —Charles Dickens

It is often overlooked that managers need good communication skills to help employees improve their productivity. The "telling and selling" approach to the performance-appraisal interview is easier for managers, but not as effective as "listening and helping." It is important for managers to recognize accurately to what extent they are helping another person plan performance-improvement. If communication is not open, honest, and mutual, the performance-appraisal meeting will not be as productive as it should be. There are four steps essential to conducting a successful performance-appraisal meeting:

Preparing for the meeting

Getting started (Stage 1)

Discussing duties, goals, and behaviors (Stage 2)

Reaching a closing agreement (Stage 3)

Meeting Preparation (usually done several days in advance)

Write down ideas on job duties, goals and behaviors.

A day or so before the meeting, explain to the employee what the meeting is for, and suggest that he/she think about the subject.

Collect all related information.

Decide how the meeting should be conducted.

This chapter is based on the work of Dr. Gerard Egan and his book *The Skilled Helper: A Model for Systematic Helping and Interpersonal Relations* (Monterey, Calif.: Brooks/Cole, 1975).

The Meeting

Getting Started (Stage 1)

> Begin informally with small talk.
>
> Ask for questions to clarify the purpose of the meeting.
>
> Reach agreement on steps, length, and other procedures of the meeting.

Main Discussion (Stage 2)
First Meeting:

> Discuss employee's job duties, goals and behaviors.
>
> Ask for his/her ideas.
>
> Give him/her your ideas.
>
> Agree on goals and behaviors.

Second Meeting:

> Ask employee to tell you how he/she did in achieving goals and where he/she sees self relative to behavior.
>
> Give your view of the above.
>
> Compare and reach agreement.

Closing (Stage 3)

> Review agreements to confirm (agree to put in writing)
>
> Decide on follow-up
>
> Ask if employee needs any special help—agree on how you will help

Clearly these are not separate and disconnected steps; collectively they serve as a guide for planning more effective performance-improvement sessions. It is important to understand and apply specific skills in the various stages of any meeting. The remainder of this chapter will discuss the development of these skills.

Helping Others Improve

Each step of the face-to-face performance-appraisal meeting requires a different set of skills. As in the steps for conducting a productive meeting, the skills needed to help an employee improve his/her performance are not isolated entities: the use of one skill does not stop when you begin the use of the next. These skills build upon each other, as bricks do, to create the platform for a successful meeting. There are a total of eleven skills.

Getting Started	1) Physical attentiveness
	2) Observing
	3) Active listening
Exploring	4) Empathy
	5) Concreteness
Discussing Performance	6) Self-disclosure
	7) Confrontation
	8) Immediacy
	9) Exploring alternative forms of reference
Closing/Agreement	10) Planning improvement
	11) Support

The good problem solver is a perceptive communicator, carefully attending to the other person's verbal and nonverbal messages. A perceptive communicator clarifies messages by interacting with the other person, advancing communication on the basis of what is being said and understood. In touch with how his/her own thoughts and feelings may affect the other person, a good problem solver maintains an openness with the other person.

Getting Started

Physical attentiveness

Observing

Active listening

Physical Attentiveness. The meeting should be held in a comfortable work environment, one that allows the participants to give full attention to each other. In such an environment, physical attentiveness means adopting a posture of SOLE involvement with one another; this posture transmits a nonverbal communication.

    S   *Squarely* face the other person.
        This is the basic posture of involvement. It says, "I am available to

you." Turning away, or at an angle, from another person lessens your involvement.

O   Maintain an *Open* posture.
Crossed arms or legs are often, at least minimally, signs of lessened involvement. An open posture is a sign that you are receptive to what the other person has to say. It is a nondefensive posture.

L   *Lean* toward the other.
This is another sign of involvement, and it helps you to listen and pay attention.

E   Maintain good *Eye* contact.
As you speak, you should spend much of the time looking directly at the other person. This is not "eyeballing" or "staring down." Eye contact simply indicates that you are paying attention. When two people are intensely involved in a conversation, their eye contact is almost uninterrupted.

We are not suggesting that you lock yourself rigidly into the attending position just described. The important thing is to remember that your body does communicate for good or ill. If you simply remember that posture has its own subtle voice, you will eventually develop a natural posture of openness.

Observing. Just as your own posture and behavior convey a message, so do the other person's. If the other person is staring at the floor, shifting around on the chair, or biting his/her fingernails, such behavior tells you that the person is probably nervous. A good observer notices every aspect of the other person's communication through mannerisms. You should, however, be careful not to make any snap judgments. Allow some time to pass, during which you simply observe without judging. When you feel that your observations are accurate, then you can begin making tentative judgments about the other person's feelings and level of energy, as well as how the person is relating to you. Remember that these initial judgments are only tentative, and they should be checked out during further discussion.

Active Listening. Listen actively to the *whole* message given by the other person. This requires that you listen, not only to the words, but also to tone of voice, loudness, pitch, pacing, stumbling, and grunts or sighs. Nonverbal communication can reveal a hidden aspect of the spoken message. This also means that you should be aware of how you sound to the other person.
Nonverbal cues serve one of two general functions.

1. They confirm, punctuate, emphasize, or otherwise modify the verbal messages of the speaker.
2. Or, they contradict the verbal messages, and thus reveal the true message.

Care should be taken to interpret nonverbal behavior only within the total context of communication: who is talking to whom, under what circumstances, with what antecedents, on what topics, etcetera. Sometimes the same nonverbal behavior can mean different things, depending on the total context.

Finally, don't become overly preoccupied with nonverbal cues and their interpretation; words still bear the brunt of the intended message.

Exploring

Empathy

Concreteness

Effective use of the three skills just discussed should bring about feelings of openness and trust during the performance-appraisal meeting, which will increase the flow of more accurate information from the other person. Again, remember that these communication skills are not an end in themselves, nor do they stop simply because you've moved into the next stage of the meeting.

Empathy. Empathy could be defined as "attentive interaction taken one step further." It is the capacity to keenly perceive emotional signals, and from these signals gain an understanding of what it might be like to *be* the other person. If you can accurately understand another person's perspective, experience, feelings and statements, then you are empathizing with that person; you become able to look at the world through that person's frame of reference. Once you have gained such insight, it is very important that you communicate this understanding to the person. Statements such as, "Yes, I can see your point of view," will help to show your empathy. You can empathize with a person, but if you don't communicate your empathy, the other person may never realize that you do understand.

Since empathy is a human feeling, the possibility exists that it could be mistaken. Thus, it is essential that you put out feelers to confirm the accuracy of your understanding. If you say, "You feel guilty because you treated your boss roughly," and the other person responds, "Yes, I really feel rotten," then your empathy is accurate because you *understand* how the other person feels. It is important to note that empathy does not necessarily mean that you agree with the other person, only that you understand the person's point of view.

There are numerous stumbling blocks on the road to understanding and communicating empathy:

Inaccuracy. Look for cues that indicate you have misunderstood, and then work to get back "with" the other person.

Feigning understanding. Don't do it! Being genuine literally demands that you admit when you are lost and that you work to get back on track.

Rambling. As a general rule, the other person should not be allowed to ramble. Neither should you!

Getting ahead of oneself. This will retard the problem-solving process. Here, the mistake is attempting to empathize too quickly, before your understanding is complete, and before the other person is ready to hear such statements.

Failing to move ahead. Do not allow the meeting to become stuck on one unproductive point or sidetrack.

Incongruence. If the other person speaks animatedly, elatedly telling you something, and you reply in a flat, dull voice, your response is not fully empathetic. It does not match the other person's level of enthusiasm.

Jumping in too quickly. This is speaking before you've formulated your response. Most of us must learn to be patient when the other person pauses. During the pause, ask yourself: "What are the feelings here? What are the real issues?" This does not mean that you should abandon spontaneity.

Language. Speak the other person's language. Your language should be in tune with the other person, reflecting your ability to assume that person's frame of reference. In other words, don't talk over the other person's head, but also, don't falsely attempt to talk an unfamiliar slang just because the other person uses it.

Long-windedness. Your responses should be relatively frequent, but also lean and trim.

Responding to feeling or content. Accurate empathy deals with both feelings *and* content. At times, however, one may be more important than the other. If the other person is easily threatened when discussing feelings, you should start by emphasizing content, and only gradually begin to deal with feelings. Most often, you will know when a person feels uneasy discussing a certain subject, because that person's uneasiness will frequently make you uneasy.

Questions. While questions have their place, don't substitute them for accurate, empathetic responses. If a question must be asked, it should be open-ended; that is, one that cannot be answered with a yes or no. Any question should yield information that leads to a greater understanding of the other person.

Concreteness. Be concrete. A vague statement such as, "The weather is just right," could mean rain for a farmer, sunshine for a bather, or an electrical storm for Ben Franklin.

All problems, feelings, behaviors must be discussed in clear, specific terms. Unless this is done, it is difficult, if not impossible, to solve problems. Vague solutions to vague problems never lead to effective action.

Speaking in abstractions can create a counterproductive distance between you and the other person. Although it is not always possible to be completely clear when communicating with another person, obscurity is hardly a goal for which to strive.

Feelings

Vague: "Group meetings give me a hard time."

Concrete: "I feel hesitant and embarrassed whenever I try to speak my mind in a meeting. I'm afraid that no one will agree with me."

Content

Vague: "People turn me off at times."

Concrete: "I feel small and inept when other supervisors brag about their accomplishments when we're all together. I clam up, and then I feel even more alone and miserable."

A concrete statement provides more accurate information, and since it is also more readily understandable, no time is wasted trying to get around to the specific point.

Performance Discussion—Body of Session

Self-Disclosure

Confrontation

Immediacy

Exploring alternative frames of reference

The attending and responding skills cited above are primarily used to move the performance-appraisal meeting forward. This does *not* mean that these skills are discarded as the meeting goes along. Remember, this is a progressive process; the skills build on one another and fit together into a whole.

Self-disclosure. Self-disclosure is simply the willingness to share feelings, attitudes, experiences, and other aspects of yourself. Since you expect self-disclosure *from* the other person, it wouldn't be right if you weren't also willing to reveal some things about yourself. There are times during the performance-appraisal meeting when it will be helpful for the other person to know just where you stand on an issue. Of course, you don't have to reveal things about yourself that are not pertinent to the discussion at hand, nor do you have to disclose anything you consider too private.

Confrontation. In the context of a performance-appraisal meeting, confrontation is an extension of empathy; that is, it is a genuine, concretely delivered response to the other person, based on a deep understanding of that person's feelings, experiences, and behavior. The aim of confrontation is to invite a person to more carefully examine behavior and its consequences.

Since it is an invitation, it is not a demand but an offer. Maintaining the invitational character of confrontation is extremely important. Otherwise, confrontation can degenerate into accusatory, punitive, and/or recriminatory behavior, and the necessary, mutual balance of communication and respect between you and the other person will be lost. Besides, if a man has a headache, you don't have to hit him in the head to get him to examine the symptoms of a headache. There are five confrontational approaches.

1. *Factual confrontation.* Basically, this is getting all the facts straight. If the other person is dealing with data that is incorrect or information that is incomplete, you should confront the other person with the missing information or the correct data.

2. *Experiential confrontation.* When your own experiences differ from those the other person describes, or when your observation of the other person's actions doesn't square with what is being said, you should invite the other person to examine these differences with you. This should never be done in a way that makes it seem you are automatically right and the other person is completely wrong.

Undeniably, one person's view cannot be *completely* communicated to another person. People are too complex for this to happen. There are, however, certain exaggerations and misrepresentations that can sometimes keep us from communicating as fully and honestly as possible:

Discrepancies. For all of us, there are discrepancies between what we think and what we say, what we say and what we do, our views of ourselves and other's views of us, what we are and what we want to be; such a list could be endless.

Distortions. Whenever we can't, or don't, want to face things as they really are, we tend to distort them with statements such as:

"I see my stubbornness as commitment."
"I see my fearful silence as tact."

Games, tricks, and smoke screens. If we're comfortable with our delusions and profit by them, we will obviously try to keep them. If we're rewarded for playing games, that is, if we get others to meet our needs by playing games, then we will continue our games. For instance, I'll play "yes, but . . ." I'll get others to work at helping me with a problem, and then show them how invalid their offers are by saying, "yes, but . . ." to each item offered. I will have my problem solved for me, while making it seem that I solved the problem.

3. *Strength confrontation.* This is one of the most productive kinds of confrontation. Based on your observations of a person's potential abilities, you should point out the strengths, assets, and resources that the person has not yet developed or utilized. Make certain that your suggestions are realistic, that they do not overinflate the person's capabilities.

4. *Encouragement to action.* Active and assertive, skilled performance-planners are agents, doers, initiators; they are not afraid to make a positive impact on others, to call others to action. Through encouragement and example, you can lead others to act upon their situation. This is especially effective when a person has expressed a desire to act but has failed to follow through.

5. *Weakness confrontation.* This dwells on the deficiencies of the person being confronted. Although it is next to impossible to entirely avoid such confrontations, weakness confrontations are the crudest form of confrontation, preferred only by unskilled problem-solvers.

By now you may be thinking, "But what if there's nothing to confront?" That's okay. Confrontation is one of the skills that is not always necessary. If there's nothing to confront, don't worry; but if there's any problem, you must confront it.

Immediacy. Immediacy is one of the most important skills, but it is also one of the most difficult to master. It is the ability to understand and discuss what is taking place between you and the other person *right now.* Through your accurate understanding of what is taking place, you can lead the other person to a higher level of immediacy. You should try to establish discussion that takes place between "you and me," not "you and them." By focusing directly on the *immediate* interaction between you and the other person, you keep the meeting on the exact track you want it to follow. Immediate interaction must be constantly monitored, otherwise you could be failing to respond to important signals and allowing the meeting to slip off-track.

When you recognize that either you or the other person has verbalized a thought or feeling that is obstructing the meeting's forward progress, immediacy is called for at that time. What makes the use of immediacy difficult is that it often requires the application of many of the skills we have previously discussed. For example, if you see that the other person is showing hostility towards you, but is doing so in subtle, hard-to-get-at ways, you may:

Let the other person know how you are affected by such indirect communication (self-disclosure); and/or

Point out the possible deeper messages of the other's actions and communications (accurate empathy); and/or

Invite the other person to examine how you are relating to each other (confrontation).

Exploring Alternative Frames of Reference. The highly skilled manager offers the other person different ways of looking at behavior, alternatives that are more accurate and constructive than those of the other. As a simple illustration, what one person sees as witty, other people may view as biting or sarcastic; bringing this up for examination provides an alternative frame of reference for that person.

Closing/Agreement—The Action Skills

Planning

Support

The purpose of a performance-appraisal meeting is to help another person to act and work more effectively, and to solve problems. All of the foundation qualities and skills of the process are of little or no value unless the other person acts, improves, or solves the problem. That's the payoff.

Action Planning. Problems are always solved more effectively when they are approached systematically. The following outlines the important elements in action planning.

1. *Establishing priorities when choosing problems for attention.* This requires a preliminary overview of all the problems and the available resources for their solution. Preferably, this overview should be reached during the earlier stages of the performance-appraisal meeting. Once the other person has

a vision of the general problems and resources, the question becomes, "Which problems do I expend my energy on first?" Here are some of the criteria to be used when choosing.

Give priority to pressing problems and crisis situations. It is essential to tackle the most pressing or overwhelming problems immediately. Decide which problems will do the most harm if left untreated.

Choose some problem that can be handled relatively easily. If people experience even a small degree of success in handling any problem, they find reinforcement, which helps them trust their resources and gives them added energy to attack the more difficult problems.

Choose a problem that, if treated, will bring about general improvement, improvements that can positively influence areas beyond just the problem area. Some solutions yield results beyond what might be expected.

2. *Defining the performance problem: Identifying and clarifying the problem.* A problem can't be solved if it's defined in vague terms, anchored to past problems, or attributed to forces beyond the control of the person involved. The person has to accept and admit, "Yes, the problem is mine, and I am the one who has to deal with it." Even if there are others who also bear responsibility for the problem, you cannot allow the individual to believe or complain, "If those other guys would get on the ball, things would get better." It is important that the individual start to work on improving performance, regardless of how "those other guys" are performing. If a problem is stated concretely enough, it is possible to begin to glimpse the solution. You should state the problem, as concretely as possible, in terms of personal behavior that relates directly to the problem.

3. *Formulating a goal statement and establishing workable goals.* The more concretely a problem can be described, the easier it becomes to develop a set of concrete, workable goal statements. From an understanding of the current, problematic situation, you should direct the other person to make concrete statements about the desired situation that is his/her goal. Here are some guidelines to use when helping someone establish workable goals.

State the goal in a way that makes it clear and workable. Patently impossible goals should be eliminated from the start.

Make certain that the person has accepted responsibility for achieving the goal, and that the goal is not unrealistic or outside of the person's control.

Have the other person state the goal concretely. When the goal is stated concretely, one can begin to see what means are needed to achieve it.

Break each goal down into manageable units.

4. *Elaborating action programs: Take inventory of the means available for achieving established goals.* Here are two techniques:

Brainstorming, the act of looking at and listing all possibilities that come to mind, no matter how far-fetched, can be very productive. List *every* idea, without worrying about how wild it is, as this is one of the best ways to get *every* idea up for consideration.

The "scenario setting" enables the other person to project the action plan into the future and predict the results. In its simplest form, the scenario can be stated as a response to the questions: "What is the worst thing that could happen?" and "What is the best thing that could happen?" By applying it to each step in the plan, this method can produce extremely detailed projections.

You'll be able to think of other ways to take stock of resources, and different methods work best for different people. With experience, you'll be able to help the other person select the method that is best for that person, at that time, within the framework of the problem to be solved.

Sound like a lot of work? Well, consider this. Many people engaged in performance-planning overlook viable alternatives and available resources, either because they don't possess practiced information-seeking skills, or because they simply don't take the time to investigate all the possibilities.

5. *Choosing the preferred course of action: Choosing the means that will most effectively achieve established goals.* When the inventory of possibilities has become as full as it can be, the person must choose which course of action will be taken to achieve the established goals. Here are two ways to do that:

Help the person choose action programs that are in keeping with the person's values. If the action program goes counter to the person's value system, problems will be created that could be worse than the ones the person is trying to solve.

Help the other person choose practical action programs, those that have a high probability of success. First of all, help the person separate practical action programs from the impractical. Action programs are not practical if they ignore unbending environmental forces. A failure to scrutinize the environment can lead to the choice of an action program that proves useless in the face of opposing environmental forces. So, try to help the other person choose action programs that will not meet an insurmountable environmental resistance.

When choosing an action program, you should help the other person evaluate the risk involved, and help determine whether the risk is proportional to the probability of success. Four strategies that deal with the factors of risk and probability are the following.

a. The "wish" strategy allows the person to choose courses of action that *could* lead to a desired goal, regardless of risk, cost, or probability.

b. The "safe" strategy allows the person to choose secure courses of action, ones that have a high probability of succeeding, but ones that might not achieve the goal in the way or to the degree that the person desires.

c. The "escape" strategy allows the person to choose a course of action that is likely to *avoid* the worst possible result; it minimizes the maximum danger.

d. The "combination" strategy allows the person to choose courses of action that, although they involve risk, both minimize danger and increase the probability of achieving a goal in the way and to the degree the person desires.

6. *Planning the action steps: Establishing criteria for the effectiveness of action steps.* It is essential that both you and the other person be able to judge whether the action program is or isn't being implemented, and to what degree goals are being achieved.

In action programs, success is the result of detail.

Vague, unrecorded action steps just don't work!

In planning to reach a goal, each action step must have certain characteristics. Each must be:

a. related to the goal
This may be obvious, but it is often overlooked.

b. moderate
It should be small enough that the step is not frustrating, but large enough that it is not boring.

c. behavioral and active
Each step should be focused on active behavior (what the problem-solver *will* do), not passive expectations (what *should* be done).

d. measurable
The steps should be stated in terms of measurable end-results. How will the problem solver know that the task is completed? How will the problem solver know how well it's been done?

e. dated

Have specific target dates for each action step.

7. *Implementing the chosen means to achieve established goals.* The crux of the matter is following through!

Support. Once the action program is underway, the person will most likely experience some degree of success and failure, while at the same time uncover previously hidden aspects of the problem, or kinks in the actual implementation of the action program.

The highly motivated manager who is skilled in performance-planning-and-review will reinforce the other's successes and help work through the problems that arise during the action phase. This includes reviewing and evaluating progress as implementation moves forward, and it may require recycling parts of the action program through the process in the light of actual implementation.

Sometimes even the most thought out and carefully planned action programs fail because the manager abandons the other person. This is unfortunate for two reasons. First, it is at this time that many people need a great deal of support, and second, after you've put this much work into helping another person, why abandon him/her?

On the other hand, we don't want to imply that supporting a person in an action program is a long-term commitment. We're not even suggesting that you need to invest a lot of additional time in supporting the person. Rather, supporting the other person goes back to the very start of the process, and such support is expressed and maintained through your attentiveness and availability to the other person.

While we've dealt with support as a separate, post-planning step, it's easy to see that support is a necessary ingredient throughout the entire process. Frequently, the person you are helping needs support *during* the action-planning stage, especially when the action program involves behavior change.

References

Argyris, C. *Increasing Leadership Effectiveness.* New York: John Wiley and Sons, 1976.

Berne, E. *Games People Play.* New York: Random House, 1964.

Bryer, Jr., J.W., and Egan, G. *Training the Skilled Helper.* Monterey, Calif.: Brooks/Cole, 1979.

Gazda, G.M. *Human Relations Development: A manual for educators.* Boston: Allyn and Bacon, 1973.

Gilmore, J.V. *The Productive Personality.* San Francisco: Albion, 1974.

James, M., and Jongeward, D. *Born to Win: Transactional analysis with Gestalt experiments*. Reading, Mass.: Addison-Wesley, 1971.

Jourard, S.M. *The Transparent Self*. New York: Van Nostrand Reinhold, 1971.

Maslow, A.H. *Toward a Psychology of Being*. Second edition. New York: Van Nostrand Reinhold, 1968.

Maslow, A.H. *Motivation and Personality*. Second edition. New York: Harper and Row, 1970.

Ornstein, R. E. *The Psychology of Consciousness*. Second edition. New York: Harcourt Brace Jovanovich, 1977.

Rogers, C.R. *On Becoming a Person*. Boston: Houghton Mifflin, 1961.

Rogers, C.R. *Freedom to Learn*. Columbus, Ohio: Charles E. Merrill, 1969.

Watson, D.L., and Tharp, R.G. *Self-Directed Behavior: Self-Modification for Personal Adjustment*. Monterey, Calif.: Brooks/Cole, 1973.

Quiz

Helping People Improve

1. Have you solved most of the performance problems for those people working for you?

              Yes   No

   Comments:

2. Do you clearly understand how to help people improve their performance, with emphasis on the word "help?"

              Yes   No

   Comments:

3. Do you know how to get to the roots of a specific performance problem so that it will be solved, once and for all?

              Yes   No

   Comments:

Appendix 4A
Feedback: Giving and Receiving

I. *Giving Feedback*

   A. What is feedback?

      1. Feedback is the sharing of your feelings and/or thoughts about another's behavior.

      2. For our purposes, feedback is either positive or negative in valence; and it deals with content that is related to either personal characteristics or performance in skill areas.

         a. *Positive feedback* deals with behaviors that you think are effective or about which you have positive feelings.

         b. *Negative feedback* deals with behaviors that you think are ineffective or about which you have negative feelings. Note: Negative feedback is not "bad" feedback.

         c. *Personal feedback* emphasizes the sharing of feelings or personal reactions to behaviors: for example, "When you did _____, I felt _____."

         d. *Performance feedback* emphasizes the sharing of thoughts about the effectiveness of behaviors: for example, "When you did _____, I thought you were effective in _____."

Thus, there are four kinds of feedback—positive personal, positive performance, negative personal, and negative performance.

   B. Why give feedback?

      1. Give feedback to help others.

When you give any of the four kinds of feedback, you are offering valuable information to another person—information that can be useful in skill development and interpersonal effectiveness.

2. Give feedback to build and maintain closeness with others.

   a. Positive feedback helps another person feel good and increases the probability that behaviors that build closeness will be repeated.

   b. Negative feedback, while it may be painful to hear, makes it possible for people to discuss and work through a problem area, rather than avoid the problem and grow apart.

C. Pre-feedback considerations

Before deciding to give feedback, especially negative feedback, consider the following:

1. Effective feedback is intended to help, not to punish, put down, or create distance. Do you honestly want to help? If not, don't attempt feedback.

2. Giving feedback means becoming more involved with another person by sharing your feelings and perceptions. In some cases, additional time is required to discuss the feedback and deal with the feelings provoked by the feedback. Are you willing to become involved and perhaps spend some time? If not, postpone your feedback.

3. In general, feedback should not be imposed on someone who does not want it. Sometimes the receiver explicitly asks for feedback. At other times there is an implicit agreement between two people about giving each other feedback. If you do not know how the other person feels, it is O.K. to ask, "I have some feedback for you. Do you want to hear it?"

4. Effective feedback is offered at a time when the receiver appears to be ready to receive it. When a potential receiver is preoccupied or experiencing deep emotion, for example, anger, sadness, etcetera, it is usually best to postpone feedback.

5. Effective feedback is directed toward behavior over which the receiver has some control. Frustration is only increased when a person is reminded of some characteristic about which he/she can do nothing.

6. Negative feedback is enhanced by specific suggestions for improvement. Before offering feedback, ask yourself: How can this person behave more effectively?

D. Guidelines for effective feedback

Once the decision to offer feedback has been made, the way in which the feedback is given becomes important. To make your feedback as helpful as possible, consider the following guidelines:

1. Give feedback that is descriptive of what the receiver is doing, but not evaluative or judgmental about him/her as a person.

   EXAMPLES: Do not say, "You're stupid." This makes a judgment about the receiver as a person and is very likely to provoke a defensive response. A more effective piece of feedback: "I think your last response missed the intensity of Joan's feelings. You said 'irritated.' She sounded furious to me."

2. In giving feedback, share your own reaction—that is, your feelings and/or thoughts about the receiver's behavior. This helps build trust. A good way to do this is to use phrases such as, "I liked . . . ," "I didn't like . . . ," "I felt. . . . ," "I thought. . . ."

   EXAMPLES: "When you backed me up in the meeting today, I felt relieved." "I liked your response to Bill. You picked up on the sadness in his voice."

3. Be specific in your feedback, rather than general.

   EXAMPLES: What *not* to say: "Your responses have been good," "You have never . . ." or "You always. . . ." What to say: "I especially like the way you confronted Bob. Your response to him was clear and accurate, yet respectful."

4. State your feedback clearly and directly, without "beating around the bush."

   EXAMPLES: What *not* to do: "John, I have been sorta wondering, well, I have been thinking that maybe, perhaps, you know well, remember when we were sorta talking yesterday and you sorta said how you felt about me, well I sorta don't know about that, maybe." What to do: "John, when we were talking yesterday, you said you were not too sure about me. I do not understand what you mean by that."

5. Respect the person's right to make the final decisions about his/her own behavior. Don't order people around or tell them what to do.

6. Don't give a person more feedback than he/she can handle at one time. That leads to an information overload.

7. In general, give feedback as soon as possible after the behavior in question (depending, of course, on time factors and the receiver's readiness to hear the feedback).

8. In a group setting, feel free to check out your perceptions with other group members. In that situation, it is respectful to ask the

receiver: "I'd like to check out my perceptions with other group members. Is that O.K. with you?"

9. Use honest, positive feedback freely. By pointing out strengths to be capitalized on, you can help a person as much as, if not more than by, commenting on areas of ineffective behavior.

E. A feedback giver's "statement of values"

In giving (offering) feedback to another person, the following "statement of values" should be yours:

"By sharing my perceptions and feelings about your behavior, I want to help you—that is, if it is O.K. with you. I want to offer information called feedback that will be useful to you in making decisions about what you do. I want to let you know where I stand, what I like and what I do not like, not to put you off, but to build trust and closeness between us. I respect you. I acknowledge your responsibility for yourself and your right to make the final decisions about what you do and how you do it."

II. *Receiving Feedback*

A. A feedback receiver's "statement of values"

Just as there is a "statement of values" for the feedback giver, there is one for the receiver:

"I *value* what you have to say about what I do. I *want to know* how you feel and where you stand. I will listen to you and when I am unclear about what you are saying, I will ask for clarification. I intend to give you my honest reaction to your feedback in a way that conveys my respect for you. Then I will make my own decisions about how I will behave."

B. Guidelines for the feedback receiver

1. Listen to the feedback as it is given.

   Keep in mind the feedback giver's purpose and "statement of values."

2. Check it out to make sure you have heard it correctly.

3. Share your honest reaction to the feedback in a way that is descriptive of your feelings and perceptions, but not evaluative of the feedback giver.

4. In a group setting, feel free to check out the feedback you have received with other group members. Their perceptions may be similar to, or different from, those of the feedback giver.

5. Decide what you're going to do with or about the feedback that has been offered to you. Then, do it!

Appendix 4B
Why Changing Our Own Behavior
Seems Difficult

Many, if not most of us, find changes in our personal and interpersonal behavior difficult to make. By way of contrast, making changes in our professional practices, technical methods, etcetera, seems relatively easy. There are a number of reasons why changes in our behavior seem difficult at best. A few of these are:

1. The way we are now is habitual. We have programmed much of our behavior to be largely automatic. Though this was done intentionally at one time, complex and powerful habits persist until consciously changed. Yet habitual patterns reflect only partial awareness, and very little energy is needed to evoke them. Combined with a busy life, habits make it difficult for us to remember a desire to act differently.

2. The way we are now is comfortable. Whatever discomforts we experience at the present time, we tend to believe that to change our behavior would only result in more pain, more risk, more chance of failing. Thus we live in a comfort zone which often blinds us to the rich rewards and, indeed, greater security which could come from extending our repertoire of skills and experiences.

3. We *don't believe* we can change. In addition, many feel it is dishonest to act differently from what they "are." These fallacies result from not understanding that we are largely the result of what we have learned to be or have agreed to be. As adults, we can change ourselves. We cannot change other adults, though we may help them in such efforts if they wish us to do so.

4. We don't understand or take account of the resistance to change. Characteristically, when it comes to change, we frequently do not realize that there will be both facilitating forces and restraining forces. At the time of greatest resolve, we visualize the facilitating forces, the changes needed, the excitement of the hoped-for rewards. This is the classic situation which takes place on New Year's Eve. But when the time of im-

plementation (execution) arrives, insight, change, goal, and resolve suddenly fade, to be replaced by an electric awareness of the restraints—risk of failure, looking foolish, loss of status, uncertainty of others' reactions, and other sources of anticipated pain.

In view of this self-defeating cycle, we clearly need to consider the facilitating and restraining forces at the proper time (today), and make it our strategy to increase the strength of the facilitating forces and decrease the strength of the restraining forces.

5. Then there is the question of, who says we should change? If another person says you should change, and that person is coming on like a parent, then the probability of your changing is less than 50-50.

On the other hand, if you really know what you want, and then move to set goals, calculate outcomes, and visualize rewards, your chances of success are high indeed.

6. Clearly, when efforts to change go unrewarded, then it is far more difficult, if not impossible, to maintain the effort to act differently than is one's custom. A trap for the unwary is to forget that a prolonged investment of effort to change may be necessary. Others often do not instantly recognize our own changed behavior. Even when it might seem notably different to us, their perceptions and habits of relationship often persist in the face of changes we make. If this happens, it is helpful to call attention to changes we've made, without being in any way negative. Asking for positive strokes can be quite effective here.

Easing the Difficulty: Contracting for Change

For all of the above reasons, and probably more, it is greatly helpful when you want to change some aspect of your behavior to write up a contract which tangibly and explicitly expresses your change goal.

Such a contract needs to reflect the following, if it is to be useful to you.

1. Express your goal in concrete behavioral terms. Answer these questions: How will I know when I have succeeded in reaching my goal? What specific steps and actions do I undertake to reach my goal? What kind of monitoring or feedback can I arrange to get while making the planned change? What is the timing?
2. Set your goal on an adult basis, that is, make sure it is clear, situationally appropriate, manageable, and likely to succeed.
3. Do you really want the change, or are you just doing what you think is desired by others?
4. Finally, be clear in your contract as to what your reward will be if you

are successful in changing. In a contractual sense, this is the "considera-tion" for which you are willing to take the effort. As noted above, we do not make significant changes in our behavior unless there is for each of us some positive change in outcomes or consequences.

5
Productivity Improvement

S agging productivity has become a critical dilemma in this country, due to increased competition from Japan and other countries. Over the last twenty years, the United States has been far from the swiftest in the race to increase productivity (see figure 5–1). And the race is to be the swiftest.

Many American organizations now believe that the only remaining frontier for increasing productivity, and perhaps even for survival, is the ability to motivate employees to increase their output.

Organizations frequently attempt to improve productivity by increasing machine capacity, updating their technology, adjusting to the current economy, or by implementing other tangible measures. Productivity is the result of a combination of various factors, including the human dimension. Despite America's technological edge over much of the world competition, there remains a productivity lag in this country; although our technology has improved output, there has been a decline in the level of our work force's desire to excel and to produce a quality product, and this lessened desire can counter (in terms of overall productivity) some of the technological and more tangible gains. The remainder of this chapter will focus on the psychological stimuli and conditions that are needed to revitalize the slackening desire of our work force.

Human Behavior and Productivity

Unlike other animals, once human beings have met their basic needs of food, shelter and safety, they strive to achieve even more, to find new ways to do things and develop new ideas. Human beings derive a great sense of satisfaction from the process of achieving these higher goals. A large number of theories concern themselves with human productivity, but only two of them are directly applicable to the actual problem of increasing the output of the American work force. The first that will be presented is the work of David McClelland, and the second was conceived by Richard E. Walton.

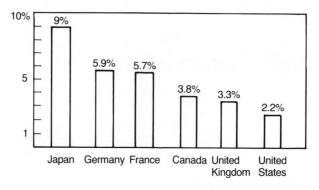

Figure 5–1. International Productivity Growth over the Last Twenty Years

David McClelland, a well-known psychologist at Harvard University, has spent his lifetime studying "the achievement drive" in human beings. Essentially, his work focuses on the theory that all people have an innate desire to achieve, some more strongly than others. He points out that Americans, as a whole, display a very strong desire to achieve.

In his search for a better understanding of the achievement drive, McClelland conducted a variety of experiments. In one of these, he asked groups of people to pitch pennies. The goal of penny pitching is to get the penny to land as close as possible to the wall. McClelland observed that when a person became consistently able to land the penny near the wall, the person would take a few steps back from the original position, thus creating a new challenge. From this new position, at a distance from which it was still possible to land the penny near the wall but which would require practice to develop consistency, the person would resume pitching pennies. Even in something as simple as pitching pennies, the achievement drive is present.

As was mentioned in chapter two, McClelland notes that there are seven basic practices which managers can employ to arouse the achievement drive in people. Please note the relationship of these seven items to the process of goal-driven management. Once again, the achievement drive can be aroused in people when the following conditions are met.

1. Specific goals are as clearly defined as possible.
2. Specific goals are achievable, but at the same time present a challenge to the individual.
3. The specific goals can be adjusted: raised if originally set too low, or lowered if originally set too high.

4. Individuals are given feedback concerning where they stand in relation to achieving specific goals.

5. The individual has accepted full responsibility for achieving the specific goals.

6. The individual knows that if a specific goal is achieved, a specific reward will be received, and that if the goal is not achieved, no reward will be received.

7. There is a climate of mutual support, encouragement and understanding.

When a manager works to bring about these seven conditions, the net result is that the individuals will experience an overall sense of achievement, and the individuals will be greatly motivated by this sense of achievement.

Techniques Used to Improve Productivity

In this country, a large variety of techniques are currently used to stimulate the achievement drive. All of these techniques have one thing in common: they use the goal-setting process as part of the methodology.

Quality of Worklife Programs: Work Restructuring*

This method, designed by Harvard's Dr. Richard E. Walton, was developed in response to the pervasive social forces that have made it necessary to improve the quality of worklife for employees in the United States. He points out five specific social influences:

1. The level of education is rising: because job-skill requirements have become more demanding, employees are bringing more extensive educations to the workplace, and their level of education often exceeds the demands of the positions they were hired to fill.

2. The need for job security is increasing: in today's uncertain environment, employees need to know that it is their performance that will determine their future (for example, that they will not be laid off, that their jobs will not be eliminated out from under their feet, etc.).

3. The emphasis on obedience to traditional forms of authority has decreased.

---

*Material abstracted from Section 6 of a productivity manual prepared for General Motors by Dr. Richard E. Walton.

4. Emphasis has shifted away from individualism towards more of a social orientation (e.g., a commitment to the other members within an organization).

5. The aforementioned decline in our work force's motivation has not been reversed.

Walton points out that, as a rule, previous approaches (job-enrichment, participative decision-making, sensitivity training, productivity bargaining, etc.) have proved inadequate in their attempts to improve today's worklife environment (thus failing to increase motivation or productivity); he further states that goal-driven management, in and of itself, is insufficiently suited to deal with this particular dilemma. Walton calls for a program of work re-structuring, and he asserts that the primary features of any such program must involve the following three elements:

1. Self-managing work teams
2. Assigning whole tasks to the individual
3. Flexibility of work assignments

Self-Managing Work Teams

The strict notion of one person/one job is deemphasized, and in its place is established the concept of creating work teams that take *collective* responsibility for a *set* of tasks, as well as responsibility for some self-management. The size of the team depends on the nature of the tasks involved. A typical team would consist of approximately seven to fifteen members: it would be large enough to perform a compatible set of interdependent tasks, yet small enough to allow *face-to-face* meetings (for decision-making, coordination, etc.). It is the unique power of face-to-face contact that can really make these teams successful; face-to-face contact provides team members with social satisfaction and individual identification (members feel they are each a necessary part of something positive), and it also facilitates the development of the capacities needed for self-management. The concept of self-managed work teams is well matched to the concepts of whole tasks and flexibility.

Assigning Whole Tasks to the Individual

According to this concept, work that has been fractionated into simple operations is reorganized into more meaningful wholes that require more operator knowledge and skill. For example, an individual worker might assemble whole carburetors, rather than adding one small part to an unfinished carburetor as it moves quickly through a work station. In continuous-process departments, whole tasks could involve a worker's comprehension of and attention to major segments of the overall process. More significantly, tasks are made whole by incorporating functions that were previously performed by other service/control units.

Most often, it is work teams that assume the responsibilities for whole tasks. The responsibilities of an assembly work team could expand to encompass new tasks such as:

a. Inspecting and maintaining quality-control of the team's own work/product (often eliminating the need for inspection from the outside)

b. Performing the needed maintenance of their own machines

c. Adjusting their own machines to accommodate whatever process was to be performed

d. Keeping house (custodial work) in their own area (especially where contamination of product is a critical concern)

As a work team's responsibilities expand, its tasks become more whole. The important thing is that the work team becomes responsible for almost every aspect of its immediate tasks, and in all cases, whole tasks are designed to include planning, as well as implementation (although the extent of allowed planning responsibility varies widely). For example, the responsibility for planning a plant shutdown for maintenance might be assumed by a work team, whereas in the past such a planned shutdown was the responsibility of management.

For a brief case study, let's examine the assembly department at Volvo. At first, short planning/reporting meetings, involving all thirty of the department's employees, were conducted every morning; rotating coordinators took special responsibility for planning, and the planning concerns allowed to the workers were initially limited to the workers' individual, daily activities. After six months, the workers' planning effectively embraced the goals of the complete thirty-person department, and workers' planning had expanded into a one week time span. A year later, workers' planning still effectively involved the entire department, but it had expanded into planning for a month's time. After three years, worker planning had progressed to the point that it included five departments (the assembly department, plus four others that were brought into the system), and workers' planning extended over a three-month time span.

Specific members of the teams are sometimes allowed to perform nontraditional, rewarding tasks such as:

a. Participate in consultation teams

b. Assume roles traditionally reserved for managers

c. Head the plant safety committee

d. Deal with outside vendors

e. Exchange documentation with ship officers

f. Investigate or trouble-shoot customers' problems

Social psychology reaffirms the need for whole tasks. In making tasks whole, the opportunity is provided for individuals to accept a challenge that both motivates and confirms the individual's self-worth.

Flexibility of Work Assignments

Flexibility is shown by:

a. Temporary reassignment from one position to another, to cover for absences

b. Temporary redivision of work, in order to handle a cluster of tasks with different sizes of workforces

c. Progressive movement from one set of tasks to the next, in order to master an increasingly larger segment of all functions involved in the work team's responsibilities

d. Systematic rotation through a series of positions

The obvious advantage of flexibility is that it allows the effective use of available manpower, and it promotes individual skill development. This mutual learning helps reinforce coordination and team-wide planning activities. The work team can usually decide how its members rotate through (and learn) a larger set of tasks.

Thus, the three aforementioned elements constitute an internally consistent scheme for the division of labor. Teams make it possible to put together whole tasks, and identification with the team's whole task provides an incentive for individuals to learn all of the interrelated jobs. In turn, flexibility allows immediate decision-making for cohesive, self-managing teams. Rotating personnel is likely to offer psychological gains (such as variety and learning) that outweigh the costs (such as uncertainty) when a whole task is self-managed by a group, rather than controlled by a separate authority.

Walton points out three secondary features that are also important.

1. The nature of the supervision is a democratic supervisory approach.

2. Information systems provide direct feedback to the individual team.

3. Reward systems are used for compensating and otherwise providing incentives for individuals and teams.

Please note how consistent Walton's observations are with those of David McClelland.

The actual operation of a quality worklife project varies immensely from one organization to another. In essence, the need for such a project can be summarized in simple terms: American management is moving away from traditional methods of managing. The traditional method (tight/direct control, strict assignments, very little feedback, etc.) allows for little or no initiative on the part of the individual and asks a person to perform relatively simple and mundane types of tasks. Most detrimentally, these methods require the individual to accomplish only very narrow and uninteresting parts of the whole job, such as putting a lug on a wheel.

In work restructuring from the very beginning individuals work in teams. They are involved in the goal-setting process, and they determine what their targets will be—how fast will they work, what will they produce, how long should they take to produce it, and so forth. Individuals have control over their work, and they are asked to perform a variety of tasks, not just one. Individuals are responsible to one another for their work and are rewarded when their work is successfully accomplished.

Notice the significant differences between the old, American system and the work-restructuring process. Obviously, each evokes a different feeling from the employee: a feeling of participating in the management of his/her job, instead of feeling controlled by the boss.

Walton suggests that there are seven conditions favorable to a pilot work-restructuring project.

Seven Conditions Favorable to Pilot Project Implementation

1. Typically, small towns provide a community context and a work force that is more amenable to the innovation. Half of the experiments were implemented in this location type.

2. Smaller work forces make individual recognition and identification easier. Half of the initial experiments involved fewer than 100 employees.

3. It is easier to change employees' deeply ingrained expectations about work and management in a new-plant culture. About half of the experiments were in situations of substantial "newness."

4. Physical separation of the experimental unit from other parts of the firm facilitates the development of a unique plant culture. Such separation assumes that the group develops its own approach and solution to problems without influence from other groups. Advantageous geographic separation appeared to be a factor for the pet food plant, the refinery, and the assembly plants of Nobo and Corning.

5. The use of outside consultants as change agents provides objectivity and know-how to the experiments. The majority of the firms had a pattern of using outside consultation in organization development, knowing how to use this type of assistance, and not being subject to criticism.

6. The long lead times that are implicit in start-ups allow large blocks of time for training and acculturation. This was a significant factor in several cases.

7. Where there is no union, or where union-management relations are positive, it is much easier to introduce the type of work systems studied. The seven unionized plants had positive union-management relations when the experiment was undertaken. Here, the parties typically agreed to a "sheltered" experiment, in which the normal contract provisions and practices were relaxed for a limited time period, and the changes were not to set precedents for other units, and that the experimental unit would return to its earlier pattern in the absence of mutual consent.

Quality Circles

Quality circles is another technique that originated in the United States, but moved to Japan, and is now moving back to the United States. People who do similar work meet regularly in small groups to identify and analyze problems and recommend solutions to management (and when possible, implement the solutions themselves). The objectives of such circles are usually to improve the quality and productivity of an organization (for example, reducing scrap and rework, improving scheduling, improving quality of the product, improving employee training, changing approaches and techniques, etc.). From this comes personal development for the individual, increases in quality and productivity, increases in morale, and hopefully better leadership.

The structure of a quality circle includes circle members (participants), a circle leader, circle facilitator, steering committee, management and nonmember advisors. Usually the circles have from eight to ten members; the members volunteer to participate in the circle. A typical quality circle meeting is held for approximately one hour per week. The first ten minutes are used to review what took place in the previous meeting, twenty minutes for new material, and thirty minutes for problem solving.

All quality circles require training for management, facilitators, leaders, and all members. The characteristics of a successful quality circle include the building of strong group-dynamics, strong group-involvement, voluntary participation, creativity, and the support from top management.

The flow of the quality circle problem-solving sequence moves like this: 1) identify the problems; 2) select the problem that the circle is to address; 3) analyze and diagnose the problem; 4) select from the various solutions and make a specific recommendation to management; 5) management accepts or rejects the recommendation; 6) implement the chosen decision(s). This flow is shown graphically in figure 5–2.

Typically, the success of a quality circle is measured by quality improvements, cost reductions, and attitude changes. Throughout the process of working with a quality circle, the goal-setting process is ever present. The

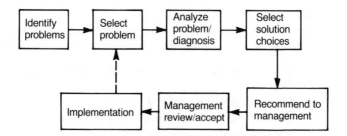

Figure 5–2. Steps in Flow of Problem/Solution

primary tool of each circle is a goal aimed at achieving or solving a selected problem, and such problems are identified by the circle itself. The net result will be improvement in some aspect of the organization's performance.

In working with their clients, Modern Management, Inc., suggests a four-stage approach to use of quality circles, as described below.

Phases of the Modern Management* Approach to Quality Circles

Stage I: *Organizational Assessment*

Through individual interviews and group meetings, the Modern Management consultants:

1. Determine the best approach to quality improvement
2. Help top management to clarify program goals
3. Work with management to select advisory committees
4. Select program facilitators

Stage II: *Orientation and Training*

In large meetings and small seminars, Modern Management consultants:

1. Orient upper-level management to the quality circle concept
2. Train program facilitators
3. Train circle leaders
4. Orient employees to the program
5. Select and train circle participants

---

*David J. Rittof, Modern Management, Inc., 11N. Skokie Highway, Lake Bluff, IL 60044, (800) 323-1331 or (312) 945-7400. Reprinted with permission.

Stage III: *Implementation and Communication*

With Modern Management consultants observing and advising the participants, the organization implements to the program by:

1. Conducting an employee attitude survey to gather baseline data
2. Conducting initial meetings
3. Distributing meeting-results through the quality circle network
4. Implementing circle contributions
5. Communicating to employees any changes made
6. Providing public recognition to participants

Stage IV: *Assessment*

Approximately eight months after implementation of the program, Modern Management consultants work with management to assess the impact of the program. Specifically, they:

1. Conduct an employee attitude survey to gather comparative data
2. Meet with facilitators, leaders, and participants to discuss their experiences and to process survey results
3. Adjust the system to maximize its effectiveness
4. Assist in expanding the system to include new areas of the organization

Participating/Problem-Solving Teams

Such teams are usually formed to involve a joint labor/management structure. Their purpose is to identify specific problems of the organization, to establish goals for solving these problems, and then to implement the plan which has been designed by the team.

Such teams are used extensively in the steel and basic industries. The underlying concept is that individuals' participation in the actual problem-solving process is highly motivating and stimulating to each individual; they feel a sense of achievement and involvement. A health care organization has gone so far as to actually identify the characteristics of successful participation, and this organization has trained their managers to perform in a manner that gives individual members of the organization a sense of involvement and participation. The actual degree to which participation is encouraged by managers is then measured by the organization in terms of improvements and changes. Although this situation is not strictly related to the goal-setting process, it does involve the manager asking employees to take an active role in the establishment of goals and the achievement towards those goals.

Other Forms of Goal Setting Directed At
Improved Productivity

Given the basic notions that people are goal oriented, and that achievement can be stimulating to individuals, it behooves the manager to look for ways to stimulate the employees' involvement in the goal-setting process. Whatever method the manager chooses to get people involved in setting their own goals, the method should lead to increased motivation and a sense of achievement. Give it any name you like, the basic principles apply.

We ask you to think about how you would feel if you were given no opportunity to be involved, no say in the methods which are used to complete work, no direct feedback, and no way of knowing whether you had done the job well or not.

The art of managing is the art of using basic human principles to help individuals feel that they are achieving their objectives and goals, both at work and in their lives.

Quiz

Productivity Improvement

1. Do you know whether your people are goal oriented and have a strong desire to achieve what they say they are going to do?   Yes   No

   Comments:

2. Do you know how to set goals so that people can reach their highest achievement levels?   Yes   No

   Comments:

3. Have you found ways to release the creativity, innovation, and skills of people in order to improve productivity?

   Comments:

       Yes   No

4. Is productivity a problem for you?

   Comments:

       Yes   No

6
Managing Cost Containment

> Value is the life-giving power of anything; cost, the quality of labor required to produce it; price, the quality of labor which its possession will take in exchange for it.
>
> —John Ruskin

As organizations grow, they have a tendency to expand to such a level that it becomes difficult to identify the functions, contributions, and interworkings of the various units. Individual managers frequently gauge their advancement in terms of the number of programs they run, size of their staff, and the degree to which they control a significant "chunk" of the organization, but not in terms of the economic contribution being made by their unit.

However difficult it is to see the broader perspective, the bottom line is that cost containment is essential to the long-range life of an organization. Goal-driven management, because of its unique goal-setting characteristic, can effectively be used to contain costs. In this case, instead of expressing a goal in terms of a behavioral change, the goal is expressed in terms of cost containment: to reduce costs by X percent, or to drop a product line because it is unprofitable. To successfully link goal-driven management to cost containment, two factors are essential.

1. Managers must assume a positive attitude. They must not think of the goal as something imposed upon them just so the organization can meet a broader set of cost-goals; instead, managers should recognize that the goal will lead to a better management of their units.

2. Any goal-setting process which is aimed at reducing or containing costs requires creativity on the part of each manager. This means finding innovative approaches to getting the job done. It is tempting for managers to say, "Give me two more people, and I'll do the job for you," or, "Give me the additional budget that I need, and I'll be able to accomplish what you want me to." It is difficult for many managers to think in terms of, "How can I do it without adding additional costs to the organization?" Successfully managed organizations, as well as successful managers, are those that are innovative, creative, and think of ways to do things that do not increase costs.

An Illustration of Cost Containment

A number of years ago, while working in the recruiting department of a large chemical company, I was asked to increase my performance. In anticipation of expansion, the company wanted to recruit 110 college students, thirty more than the goal of the previous year. The standard way of dealing with this increased goal would be to add additional manpower and recruit at additional schools. I went to my immediate boss and recommended a budget increase of approximately twenty percent, to cover travel costs and increased manpower. His response was, "Go back to the drawing board and find a way to do it without increasing your costs." Given the situation we faced, this was no easy task.

We came up with four possible approaches. The first was to reduce budgets in other areas and transfer the money to the recruiting area. A second approach was to increase our "batting average" by interviewing the same number of people but getting a greater number of them to accept our offer. The third approach was to lower our standards and accept people we would not have accepted in the past. The fourth approach, which was the one that best suited our needs, was to utilize those managers, working in other departments at the time, who had requested an opportunity to gain experience in the recruiting field. This approach grew out of the "individual development planning for managers" process, designed to provide development opportunities for high-potential managers. As a result, we were able to borrow manpower and double up on our travel expenses, and there was no significant cost increase. At the same time, we gave managers the opportunity to gain experience in recruiting. This innovative approach was successfully implemented.

Steps in the Cost Containment Process

The following steps were presented by Henry Migliore and Roger Fritz at the International MBO Conference in 1978.[1] These steps will help you apply goal-driven management concepts to cost containment.

Step 1   Top management should fully endorse cost containment as an integral part of each manager's job, and each manager must realize the importance of cost containment to successful managing.

Step 2   Top management should establish a cycle of planning sessions, to be held at designated intervals, for the purpose of setting and reviewing goals.

Step 3   Brainstorm to generate a list of all possibilities for avoiding, controlling, or reducing costs, and then rank these possibilities according to their potential savings to the organization. Each manager should submit not only the goal, but also this complete list of the alternatives that have been generated.

Step 4   Conduct a detailed cost analysis, and maintain a management system that will keep track of the progress made towards each of the various goals.

Step 5   To make certain that one unit's goals are not detrimental to, or in conflict with, another unit's, managers from the various units should meet. This will also provide an opportunity to establish goals that more than one unit might work towards, or to eliminate any unproductive, overlapping goals.

Step 6   When examining the complete list of possibilities for containing costs (from Step 3), focus on those possibilities which present the highest potential for savings, while making certain that any potential savings will be more valuable than any potential adverse effects upon performance if a specific possibility were to be acted upon. Select those possibilities that will produce the greatest savings, but which will not handicap high-priority projects, and set specific goals to realize those possibilities. If the company is experiencing economic difficulties, eliminate all low-priority projects.

Step 7   Require each manager or task team to design a plan of action for achieving a chosen goal.

Step 8   Require the establishment of a feedback system for each major cost-containment goal. The lack of a feedback system will decrease the managers' interest in achieving the goal, since they will have no comprehensive way to know whether they are succeeding or failing.

Step 9   When setting cost-containment goals for a specific year, each manager musk keep in mind how these goals will influence performance in the future. Each manager must be able to answer the question, "Will this goal be beneficial in the long run?"

Step 10   The behaviors and attitudes of all managers, from the highest level to the lowest, must coincide with the organization's overall goal of cost containment. Top management cannot be extravagant. No limousines, thank you, when we're trying to keep down costs.

An example of an overall strategy for cost containment is shown in figure 6–1. This depicts the integration of all aspects of management as they relate to cost reduction.

When integrating cost containment into the overall strategy of goal-driven management, it is essential that such integration be uniformly implemented throughout the entire organization. If only one or two units are expected to contain costs, those units' managers will think, "Why should I give up anything, if no one else plans to do the same. I'm already operating with inadequate resources."

Cost-Containment Programs[2]

Typically, a cost-containment program should be initiated in order to maintain resilience and flexibility in a constantly changing economy. At its core, a cost-containment program is one that increases productivity, a need so great that the United States government has established the National Center for Productivity and Quality of Working Life.

Communications. A philosophy of work improvement must be communicated to all levels of management and labor to assure success of the program. The expected benefits and goals should be specified so that understanding and appreciation will lead to shared enthusiasm and a better employer-employee relationship. Emphasis should be placed on achieving goals of better and faster service through lower costs of materials and labor.

Suggestion Systems. For a cost-reduction program to be fruitful, top management should initiate and completely support all channels and procedures for an ongoing employee suggestion system, for the employee often has the best view of what could stand to be changed. A responsible review committee, with authority to reward and implement worthy suggestions, can cut across departments and across levels of management, in order to elicit participation.

Training of employees by industrial engineers in the techniques of value-analysis and creativity can be helpful to implant awareness of possible improvements and to establish a receptive climate for suggestions. Specialized forms (see figure 6–2) that compare present and proposed method(s) and indicate estimated cost-savings can simplify the suggestion procedure.

Successful Programs. The National Center for Productivity and Quality of Working Life, in a monograph of December 1975, found that in companies successfully utilizing programs to improve productivity, a pattern emerged: top management supported the effort; the key role of the company's employees was recognized; the purposes and goals of the productivity-improvement program were understood at all levels; goals were developed, and standards

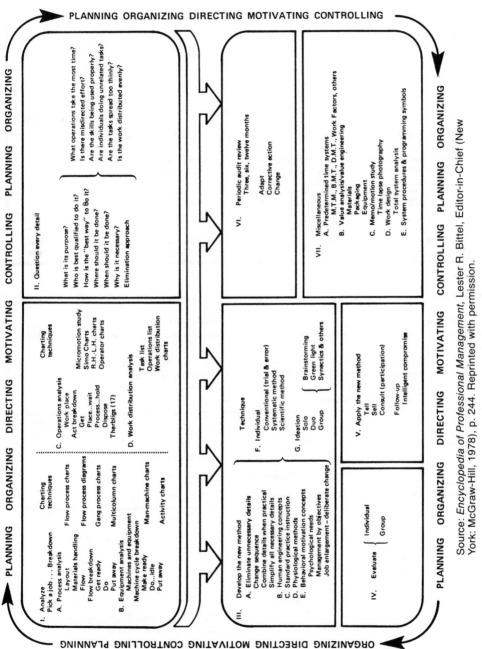

Source: *Encyclopedia of Professional Management*, Lester R. Bittel, Editor-in-Chief (New York: McGraw-Hill, 1978), p. 244. Reprinted with permission.

Figure 6–1. Example of a Strategy for Cost Containment

COST—REDUCTION REPORT

DESCRIPTION OF ITEM INVOLVED
    DEPT.   Finished stock & shipping
    OPERATION Marking with name and address of cosignee
    OBJECT OF ANALYSIS To determine possible savings through stamping instead of stenciling

FILE   11-B
DEPT. NO.   64   DATE
PRODUCT Cartons to be shipped

Comparison

Present method		Proposed method	
Machine		Machine	
Tools: Fountain stencil brush and precut stencil		Tools: Rubber stamp and stamp pad	
Description: Stencils are prepared in advance and kept on file for all major cosignees, and name and address are stenciled on each carton		Description: Rubber stamps would be made up for all major cosignees, and name and address are stamped on each carton	
Cost of operations involved:	$ per	Cost of operations involved:	$ per
Labor	carton	Labor	carton
0.16 minute per carton @ $3.00 per labor-hour	0.0080	0.05 minute per carton @ $3.00 per labor-hour	0.0025
Materials		Materials	
Miscellaneous		Miscellaneous	
Total of above items	0.0080	Total of above items	0.0025

Estimate of savings:
    Saving with proposed change ($0.0080 − $0.0025) equals $0.0055 per carton
    Probable yearly requirements 1,250,000 cartons   Estimated by   Sales dept.
    Estimated savings per year (based on 1,250,000 per year) $6875.00

Estimated cost of change:		Probable savings per year $6500.00
Design $ est. by		Less total cost of change . . . . $ 500.00
Equipment $500 " "		Net savings first year $6000.00
Installation $ " "		New method would pay for itself in months 1
$ " "		
$ " "		Note: 100 rubber stamps required at $5.00 each
Total cost		
of change $500.00		Suggested by John Ryan
		Report prepared by T. A. Wilson

cc to	Attached are		Date	Date
	1 Sheets drawings	First considered	Expen. appr.	
	Sheets prints	Investgn. started	Installed	
	2 Sheets details	Rept. submitted	Final rept.	

Source: Ralph M. Barnes, "Cost Reduction Report," *Motion and Time Study,* 6th ed., p. 39. Copyright © 1968 John Wiley & Sons, Inc. Reprinted with permission.

Figure 6–2. Example of a Cost-Reduction Report

of success were established to measure whether, and to what extent, the goals were being met; and productivity improved to the extent possible without impairing job security.

Although company approaches differ, Beech Aircraft Corporation typifies what an all-out program of cost reduction can accomplish. The overall improvement program at Beechcraft is under the direction of the cost-control management. The budget for each phase must be procured from savings from the previous period. A work-simplification administrator has plant-wide responsibility to organize, train, direct, and follow up the program. Training in work simplification techniques makes all employees aware of the possibilities of job improvements. After employees learn the basic tools, they achieve results that amount to as much as a half-million dollars a year. Beechcraft also has a separate suggestion program, headed by its own administrator, with monthly and semiannual awards made by a committee reviewing and evaluating the suggestions. A strong program of goal-driven management, with work measurement for control standards, is another factor in Beechcraft's successful cost-containment programs.

Cost containment should be a constant concern, not some last-hope consideration brought up only when the company is in trouble, or the economy is sliding into a recession. Each manager must come to recognize that cost containment is a constant consideration. If not, there might not be many tomorrows for the organization.

Notes

1. Reprinted with permission of Dr. Henry Migliore, Oral Roberts University, Tulsa, Ok.

2. Lester R. Bittell, Editor-in-Chief *Encyclopedia of Professional Management* (New York: McGraw-Hill, 1978), p. 244.

Quiz

Managing Cost Containment

1. Have you been successful in getting your staff to use   _____   _____
    goals as a means for cutting costs?   Yes   No

    Comments:

2. Have you been able to get people to link their goals clearly to budgets as well as to long-range plans?

    Yes   No

Comments:

3. Does your reporting system make people working for you keenly aware of their costs, so they know exactly how to correct cost-related problems?

    Yes   No

Comments:

4. Is cost containment uppermost in the minds of people working for you when they set goals?

    Yes   No

Comments:

7
Strategic Planning

> We never know how high we are till we are called to rise and then,
> if we are true to plan, our statures touch the skies.
> —Emily Dickinson

From its initial application as a performance-appraisal tool, goal-driven management has developed into a broader system of managing, and it is now linked to strategic planning. The basic difference between goal-driven management and strategic planning is the kinds of goals each system is designed to meet; while goal-driven management goals are very specific and oriented towards more immediate results, strategic goals are broader in nature and oriented towards results that might not be realized for five or ten years. Strategic planning helps give the organization a sense of direction, and it also provides the methods for keeping the organization on its chosen path. Without strategic planning, the external environment (a shrivelling market, increased competition, an economic recession, etc.) and internal forces (outdated or unworkable philosophies, obsolescent equipment, decreased productivity, etc.) can interact to change the direction of an organization, and this undesired change might not be realized until it's too late.

If strategic goals are viewed through the eyes of "what's going on this month," they will not be seen clearly; strategic goals are clear only when they are viewed through the eyes of "where will the organization stand in ten years." For example, an organization might set a goal to penetrate a new market by twenty percent over a five-year period. The strategy for this goal would then be divided into a series of substrategies that would designate the specific manner in which the organization plans to penetrate the market. This hypothetical organization's strategy might be to introduce into the market a product that has characteristics that no other product has, and then to attract the market by emphasizing the product's unique features. Clearly, the success or failure of such a strategy could not be adequately evaluated until the end of the designated five-year period.

At this point, it seems appropriate to present a more concise definition of strategic planning:

> Strategic planning is the process of determining what the broader
> goals will be for an organization and establishing plans of action,

policies, and practices which will govern the organization's movement towards these broader goals over a long-range period of time.

Strategic plans are usually based on three fundamentals:

1.   The socioeconomic conditions within which the organization functions
2.   The values and philosophy of the organization's top management
3.   An analysis of the organization's strengths and weaknesses

These fundamentals are not isolated from each other, and each has an influence upon the development of a strategic plan. This interaction is illustrated in figure 7–1.

It is easier to see how, on the personal level, these fundamentals can influence plans. For instance, if your long-range plans include the completion of a college degree in engineering, you must consider these three fundamentals:

Socioeconomics. Will you be able to afford tuition, and do your work and/or family obligations allow you the time needed to attend classes and study?

Values. How important is the completion of the degree to you and to the direction you want your life to take?

Strengths and weaknesses. Are your abilities such that you will be able to successfully complete the degree?

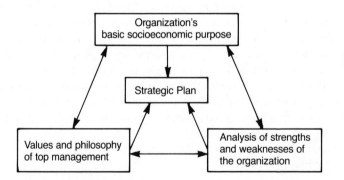

Figure 7–1. Model of Interactions of Factors Affecting Strategic Planning

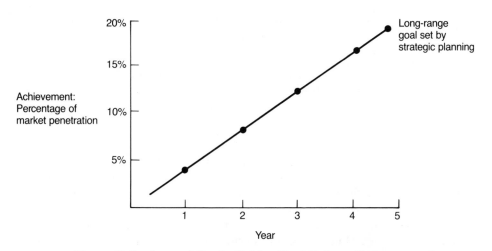

Figure 7–2. Annual Goals Set by Goal-Driven Management

Your responses to these questions will help you to decide whether your long-range plan is feasible. Strategic planning at the organizational level is very similar to that conducted on the personal level only the concerns, goals, and fundamental considerations are those of an organization.

The broad, strategic planning is usually determined by top management, and the short-term, annual planning is usually the responsibility of middle and lower management.

Figure 7–2 shows that strategic planning outlines the broad goal, and the goal-driven management process divides the long-range strategy into specific, annual goals, thus providing a means to evaluate achievement of the broader goal. Annual goals, set by goal-driven management, act as a sensing mechanism to tell how the strategic goal needs to be modified. Strategic planning ensures that annual goals will be set with a more precise understanding of the overall direction.

Advantages of Strategic Planning

1. Strategic planning forces an organization to *anticipate* any possible, future changes in its environment; an organization can no longer assume a "wait and see" attitude.

2. Once an organization knows the *direction* in which it desires to move, it becomes clear what specific, short-term goals need to be established to reach the desired destination.

3. By providing the opportunity for people to rally around specific goals and to marshal their resources towards achieving these goals, strategic planning establishes a basis for *teamwork*.

4. Strategic planning helps management learn to *cope* with the increasingly ambiguous nature of today's organizational world.

The Four Elements of Strategic Planning

1. *Definition of the organization and its purpose.* In order for an organization to determine its direction, it has to understand exactly what it is trying to accomplish, both today and in the future. The organization must remember how it got where it is today, but it must also project where it will stand in the future. For example, the K corporation has been manufacturing typewriters for decades, but it must now decide whether or not it should attempt to penetrate the home-computer market. They got where they are by making typewriters, but can they get to where they want to be by staying with typewriters only?

2. *The organization's driving forces.* An organization must take stock of its new ideas and available resources. If the K corporation has developed an innovative technology that is not yet obtainable on the home-computer market, this development would be a driving force behind the decision to penetrate the market. But, if the K corporation lacks the financial flexibility to support this new venture, the possibility becomes flawed. An organization must understand every aspect of what makes the organization tick, and must measure each aspect in relation to the other.

3. *The current position of the organization.* An organization must recognize where it stands in relation to its market. A well-established organization already has a reputation and a fairly strong sense of direction, while a newcomer must decide upon its direction and forge a reputation for itself. The K corporation has a name in typewriters, and this *could* be transferred to the home-computer market; the X corporation must *make* a name for itself in the home-computer market. Keep in mind, a good reputation is not always an "in." For instance, an organization that was noted for being an expert buggy manufacturer would have a great deal of difficulty using that reputation to sell bicycles to today's customers.

4. *The structure of the organization.* The way an organization is structured to achieve its current goals may not be the same as the organizational structure needed to achieve future goals. There are a number of structural factors that must be considered before strategic planning is undertaken.

a. What are the various organizational inputs (raw materials, manpower, finances, etc.) currently required to make the organization successful, and what inputs will be required for success in the future?

b. An organizational profile should be prepared, and this profile should focus on the strengths and weaknesses of the organization, while keeping in mind the viewpoint of the individuals within the structure.

c. Is the current organizational structure responding to the socioeconomic environment surrounding it, and is it flexible enough to anticipate the changes that will transpire within its environment?

d. Conduct a research audit to determine what mistakes the organization has made in the past, and to make certain that the organization will not repeat these mistakes.

e. The design of any strategy should take into account the information revealed by the organizational profile and the research audit; this information will reveal the weak areas to be improved and the strong areas to be maintained. Also, this information should indicate the feasibility of the strategy, and it can help prevent you from planning a strategy that relies too heavily on an area that might not be strong enough to carry the weight.

f. Develop alternative strategies for broadening the structure of the organization to encompass new products or services, while at the same time expanding the distribution of current products or services.

g. Along with the overall strategy, prepare a flexible feedback system; this system should be capable of correcting any faltering of, or diverging from, the overall strategy.

Steps in the Strategic Planning Process

To achieve a goal, specific steps must be undertaken: for any chosen strategy, a different set of strategic planning steps must be developed. I would like to direct your attention to two general outlines that should prove helpful when you are designing a strategic plan. The first outline was developed by Louis Allen,[1] and the second was adapted from Allen's work by Eugene J. Benge.[2]

Louis Allen proposes the following set of steps be utilized in the planning of any strategy:

1. Forecasts: predict what should be done.
2. Decisions: develop specific goals.
3. Policies: analyze the conditions required to successfully achieve goals.
4. Programs: determine steps to be followed in achieving goals.
5. Schedules: establish a timetable that specifies the way in which resources (manpower, materials, etc.) will need to be utilized to achieve goals.
6. Procedures: establish methods to be followed.
7. Budgets: determine how much it will cost.

Allen further suggests that two important characteristics of strategic planning be kept in mind throughout the process:

1. Planning is based on a set of assumptions about what will happen in the future, and you need to remember that these assumptions are not realities: on a map of the future, the roads won't always take you where they promise.
2. Since strategies are planned and carried out by human beings, strategies cannot be free from error; you must recognize and compensate for the manifestations of human imperfection.

Eugene Benge proposes only five general steps:

1. Realistically appraise the strengths and weaknesses of the organization.
2. Involve the organization's key personnel in the planning process.
3. Gear the plan towards the consumer to give it a market orientation.
4. Establish a subdivided, five-year plan, and then delegate the responsibilities for the plan.
5. Set up a schedule that indicates key milestones to be reached, and then keep to it.

Benge's steps could be thought of as "factors not to be overlooked." In particular, steps two and five deserve further attention:

Step 2.   If you expect people to be committed to the strategic plan, then they must have a hand in the planning process.

Step 5.   Often, an elaborate strategic plan is established, but it is then put on the back burner and no further attention is paid to it: the result of this is a burnt, empty pan.

Basic Rules for Keeping Strategic Planning on Target

1. The principles under which the strategic plan functions must also be followed by the planners themselves; the planners should establish goals for completing the various steps of the planning process. This will prevent strategic planning from becoming "an item to be discussed next month."
2. Remain flexible, and build flexibility into the strategic plan.
3. The strategic plan should be constantly monitored; but an organization must not panic if an unforeseen problem crops up, or if progress is lagging slightly behind expectations.

4. Consistently test the assumptions underlying the strategic plan; this will expose any faults in the logic of the plan.
5. Entrust the achievement of short-term goals to those managers who are directly responsible for the day-to-day functions of the organization.
6. Encourage all managers to be involved in the entire strategic process.
7. Don't let temporary downturns in performance scare you away from the strategic plan: don't expend an excess amount of resources to remedy a current problem at the expense of the strategic plan. You must keep in mind the outcome of the organization's past slumps and surges; the organization is sure to feel a few "growing pains." If the strategic plan is sound, short-term problems will work themselves out. In other words, don't give up on the marathon just because you develop a slight leg cramp: stop, massage the muscle, then continue on with the long race.

Notes

1. Adapted from Louis Allen as presented in the Armco. Steel Corp. film, "Planning."

2. Eugene J. Benge et al. "Management in Perspective," *SAM Advanced Management Journal* (1965), pp. 203–204. Reprinted with permission.

Quiz

Strategic Planning

1. Did your goal-driven management system start from the framework of long-range planning and lead to individual goal-setting?　　Yes　　No

    Comments:

2. Have you been successful in getting people in your organization to tie their individual goals to the long-range plan?　　Yes　　No

    Comments:

3. Do you and your staff know the steps in long-range
planning?

Yes   No

Comments:

4. Have you been successful in getting people to think
much beyond one year, as they set their goals?

Yes   No

Comments:

Appendix 7A
Questions on Strategic Planning

The purpose of this list is to enhance your thinking about strategic planning for your organization. Jot down your thoughts and use them as a springboard to examine how you are applying strategic planning concepts.

1. What is the direction/purpose of your organization?

2. What are the driving forces in your organization? What are the retarding forces?

3. Describe the socioeconomic environment surrounding your organization.

    Today

    2 years into future

    5 years into future

4. What alternatives does your organization have for:

   Expanding current products/services

   Developing new products/services

5. Weigh each alternative in terms of advantages and disadvantages, then select the most likely to succeed.

6. Evaluate your organization's competitive environment:

   Today

   2 years into the future

   5 years into the future

7. What strengths can your organization utilize to achieve strategic goals?

8. Develop a strategic statement defining future direction(s) and goal(s).

9. Design a sample annual plan to fit into the above strategic statement.

8
Developing an Organization

> Without development there is no profit. Without profit no
> development.
>
> —Joseph Alors Schumpeter

Not since the Industrial Revolution have society's attitudes about worklife undergone such an intense scrutiny; they are currently subject to an ongoing flood of articles, debates, and books concerned with the conditions required for a healthy, productive worklife. Dr. Allan Filley has described our times as the second "Great Age of Social Experimentation." Because work is central to the lives of so many Americans, work that is viewed as meaningless creates frustrations that reverberate through every fiber of our American lives. When work is viewed as meaningless, the worker feels an increasing alienation, and this sense of alienation can lead the worker to feel that it is absurd to strive to do the best job possible. It is this sense of hopeless absurdity that must be yanked out by the roots.

The first step towards improving the quality of worklife must necessarily be the commitment of the policymakers in business, labor, and government to this broad goal, but managers at every level must also be committed to improving the quality of worklife. Many managers, much to their dismay, are finding that their skills and knowledge are not suited to the fluctuating demands of today's worklife environment; consequently, many managers are now increasingly motivated to acquire the skills and knowledge required to effectively manage in this "experimental age." Working within the process of organization development (OD), managers can develop the necessary skills and knowledge.

Firmly rooted in such disciplines as psychology, communication, and sociology, organization development serves as a framework for managers, researchers, and academics alike to deal with the complexities of organizing and managing human resources. The program of organization development is a long-range effort (involving the entire organization, or a coherent system of parts thereof) to beneficially intervene in the activities of the organization, to facilitate learning, and to make decisions concerning procedural alternatives. The goal of OD is to increase an organization's effectiveness and to enhance organizational choice in self-renewal.

A Definition of Organization Development (OD)

One of the most difficult tasks of writing about organization development is defining what the process is. There are at least four well-accepted definitions:[1]

1. OD is a *planned change* effort involving the *total system* managed from the top to *increased organizational effectiveness* through planned interventions using *behavioral science knowledge.*
    (Richard Beckhart)

2. Using knowledge and techniques from the behavioral sciences, Organization Development attempts to integrate *individual needs* for growth and development with *organizational goals* and objectives in order to make more effective organizations.
    (National Training Laboratories Institute)

3. OD is a process of planned organization change that centers around a *change agent* who in collaboration with a client's system attempts to apply valued knowledge from the behavioral sciences to client problems.
    (Warren Bennis)

4. Achieving an idea of corporate excellence to strive towards and perfecting a sound system of management which can convert driving forces into action.
    (Blake and Mouton)

The key, unifying element of these definitions is the concept of *planned change.* Perpetually, many changes are taking place within every organization; unfortunately, most of these changes are met with an attitude of "let it happen as it may," and this attitude is causing serious problems in the management of our human resources. Organization development eliminates such *laissez-faire* attitudes and approaches change with the idea that major variables can be controlled in a planned and systematic manner; OD is designed to give organizations the ability to anticipate and to adapt so that changes are not random and directionless. In OD terminology, a planned change is called an *intervention.*

One of the underlying ideas of OD is to match the individuals' needs to the organization's goals. This is one of the tasks of the *change agent.* The change agent (often an internal or external consultant, or a chosen manager) serves as the catalyst or prime mover in the intervention strategy. For our purposes, think of yourself as a change agent; we believe that every manager is in some way responsible for bringing about change within the organization.

One major American corporation defines its OD program as a

> Plan for applying appropriate resources to organization revitalization. . . . It is a planned intervention in the ongoing management process with the ex-

plicit intent of applying new knowledge, new technology, new resources, and new individual organizational authenticity to the achievement of the organization's goals in a dynamic and uncertain environment. . . . [the goal is to] increase earnings now . . . [and] to do so in such a way that the organization's capacity for continued growth and earnings are within its own control. . . . [the OD program is] a means of changing the management process from one of dependence on previous experiences to one of autonomy based on the utilization of total technical and human resources.

This particular corporation does not think of organization development as an imposed program but rather as a way to manage the continued revitalization of their organization.

Goals of Organization Development

When presenting the overview, we touched briefly on the goals of a typical OD program. Although the goals of any OD effort may vary according to the situation an organization faces, we believe that organization development must adopt several major goal-orientations, such as:

1. To increase the basic organizational effectiveness and make the organization a more acceptable place for people to work
2. To build trust among individuals and groups throughout the organization
3. To create an open, problem-solving climate in which problems are confronted and differences are clarified both within and between groups
4. To locate decision-making and problem-solving responsibilities as close to the information sources and relevant sources of data as possible
5. To find ways to increase the feeling of participation that people need to experience in their organizations
6. To move toward a more participative approach to managing between individuals and groups within an organization and strive for a cooperative rather than a competitive approach
7. To increase the awareness of people concerning the processes underlying their ability to perform in the organization; to make people as aware of the organization's process as they are of the organization's tasks (if people don't understand the process, it's extremely difficult for them to accomplish the tasks)

One national organization, Saga Corporation, has an extensive organization development program and is generally cited for its successful OD effort. Saga provides a fine example of how individuals' improvement can contribute to organizational growth. Its OD goals are as follows:

1. To enable Saga people to be exposed to and acquire the human-relations skills needed to make them maximally effective human beings by fulfilling their highest personal goals in every situation, while meeting the needs of all concerned

2. To help individuals become truly aware of themselves in every aspect of their being at all times

3. To assist people in gaining knowledge and insight about the impact of their behavior—whatever it may be—at any given moment

4. To create a climate of emotional security so that individuals can talk about how they feel. Thus, feelings can be on top of the table where they can be dealt with as such, rather than remaining hidden forces that warp logic and distort judgments

5. To prompt individuals to govern their own behavior so that it becomes a conscious force for achieving goals, instead of an ungovernable force which results in actions spurred on by emotions alone

6. To encourage participants to be fully aware of how people behave, function, and feel so that they can have a better understanding of how to best use their own skills in directing their behavior and in relating to others

7. To expand each person's understanding of the realities, forces, and dynamics in every situation so that he/she can consciously apply the kind of behavior that will cause the situation to improve

8. To guide each person in formulating goals for every situation or relationship of which he or she is a part

9. To discourage individuals from viewing OD as "soft-style management" and to encourage directness and effectiveness in dealing with tough situations. The ideal OD behavior is that which is fully congruent with the situation at hand

10. To provide Saga managers and the Saga systems with methods to achieve the comprehensive nature of OD which, in reality, should be called the "Saga Way of Management."

An Overview of the OD Approach to Intervention

One of the ways to describe what happens in OD is to clarify what goals we are attempting to achieve, what we are assuming to be desirable organizational goals, and what processes we need to bring about the changes to be made. Figure 8–1 helps to explain this.

We assume that the desired goals listed in table 8–1 are common to most organizations and that the OD objectives to develop an adaptable and relevant organization are also acceptable to most managers. In its simplest form, OD attempts to improve organizational processes so that both organizational and individual goals are more readily attainable.

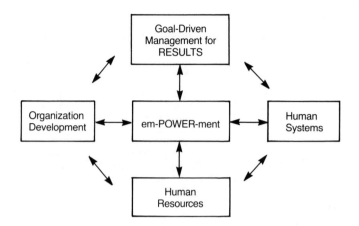

Figure 8–1. Role/Relationship of Em-power-ment in Goal-Driven Management

J. Jennings Partin identifies three characteristics of OD important to a manager:

1. The target for change is the total organization (or a large portion thereof), as opposed to an individual.
2. The goal of any OD effort should be to improve the organization's effectiveness.
3. The changes that are made should be based on a sound understanding of the concepts provided by behavioral-science models and data; a manager should not make on-the-spot changes.

Management practices *must* coherently relate to the feelings, behaviors, and tasks of the individuals within the organization.

OD concepts should not be flung into the workings of an organization; give these concepts a considerable amount of thought. A well thought out strategy for change will always enjoy a higher degree of success than the quick-fix strategy. OD is not directed towards short-term gain; its aim is to establish a lasting vitality and viability.

Don't be mistaken. We're not trying to turn every manager into a social scientist; we're only trying to help every manager understand the concepts underlying organization development.

The Linkage Between OD and Goal-Driven Management

When an organization begins to apply goal-driven management as a basic management process, the need for OD increases dramatically; the underlying

Table 8–1
Organizational Goals and Processes and OD Objectives

Desired Organizational Goals	Objectives of OD	Organizational Process Involved
Work is managed against goals. Organizational structure is developed out of function. Decisions are made near source of information (authority of knowledge as well as role). Communications are undistorted. There is high collaboration and low competition. Conflict which is inevitable is managed. A feeling of participation in change efforts. Teams are the basic unit of work. There are built-in, continuous improvement mechanisms.	To develop a viable organization that is highly adaptable and relevant to: 1. A changing environment 2. Changing needs and goals of members.	Decision-making and problem-solving Planning and goal-setting Communications Leadership and authority Cultural norms and values Intergroup relations Member values and functions

rationale for goal-driven management is a participative form of management. Managers must have the behavioral science skills needed to develop a participative program, and they must be allowed to set their own goals within the organization's overall strategy. When an organization shifts to a more participative form of management, there are a number of critical alterations involved; there is a shift from mandated goal-orientation to shared goal-orientation, and the behavior of every individual member of the organization must be directed towards participation. Both goal-driven management and OD are needed to manage these alterations.

One way to explain the relation between OD and goal-driven management has been outlined by Dr. R. S. Underhill of the University of Richmond. Figure 8–1 illustrates this connection.

The model in figure 8–1 identifies five major areas that are potential entry points for systematically approaching the workings within an organization. Two of those areas, goal-driven management and OD, have already been covered in some depth, although the goal-setting process within this context involves much more than simply writing goals. The remaining areas are closely related and support the idea that the integration of units has the greatest potential for total effectiveness. In this application, the individual is extremely important, and in these areas, we must seek to satisfy a variety of human needs.

One area, human resources, deals with the personal values and personal growth issues that develop and affirm the selfhood of the individual within

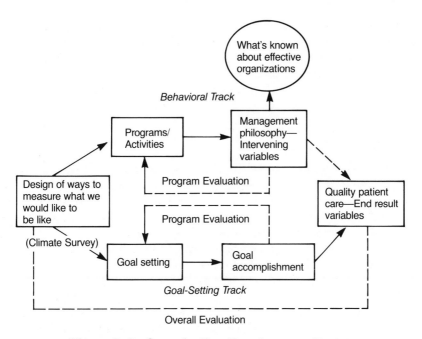

Figure 8–2. Organization Development Model

the organization. Human systems is also concerned with assuring that the systems within the organization are human-oriented. Such systems should seek to develop policies, procedures, organizational structure and operations that help individuals to achieve organizational *results* rather than just perpetuate individual activities.

The central area has to do with *power* or, more appropriately, the em-power-ment of the individual. (We have drawn primarily on the work of John Talbot, an OD consultant, for our theory base in em-power-ment diagnosis and application.) It is only through personal power that the fullest potential of the organization will ultimately be realized. This form of personal power applies a variety of OD issues to develop psychological contracts on how to use power in a way not based on hierarchical authority. As you can see in figure 8–2, empowerment is the core of the integrated system. Unless the interconnecting channels are kept open, not much flow of energy will occur in the organization.

In a broad sense, this model provides a theory base to empower the system to establish the organizational results desired, to examine the organization's development needs to maintain the process, and to achieve results through goal-driven management. Later in this section you will see how organizations have integrated OD and goal-driven management.

Dr. Wendell L. French, of the University of Washington, suggests the application of a collaborative approach to goal setting. The text of his approach is included in Appendix 8A to illustrate an integration of OD concepts with goal-driven management concepts. (Dr. French uses the term MBO, which for our purposes is essentially the same as Goal-Driven Management.)

Case Study of OD and Goal-Driven Management Integration

The practices of a medium-sized midwestern hospital (450 beds) help to illustrate how goal-driven management and OD are interrelated. At its inception, organizational development in the hospital was viewed as a way to improve the organization's performance. The model which they used to visualize the change and improvement process is shown in figure 8–2.

In this model there are two basic tracks: the behavioral track and the goal-setting track. The behavioral track deals primarily with programs and activities designed to change the behavior of managers in the organization, and it is guided by the management philosophy (also referred to as intervening variables). The management philosophy is expressed in two ways: in the criteria for an effective organization, and in a statement of management philosophy. The object of the behavioral track is to help managers understand the management approach that is advocated in the hospital and provide the means and programs to help them change their behavior. In the model you'll note a dotted line leading to "quality of patient care." The dotted line implies that an indirect relationship exists between the management philosophy/behavior and the end-result. There is no claim that a direct cause and effect relationship exists. It is assumed that a clear and human-oriented management philosophy will create a climate that will contribute to improved patient-care (measured by end result variables).

The goal-setting process contributes directly to the achievement of end results. On this track, top management establishes major-goal areas for the organization for the upcoming year. Managers are then required to establish personal goals and work-related goals consistent with the organizational goals. Some allowances are made for individual variance from these goals, depending on the tasks of the various departments. The organization strongly recommends the establishment of goals based on a set of criteria referred to as "criteria for a well-designed goal." They also encourage individuals to meet in groups within their departments to go through the goal-setting process; goals are shared to insure consistency and commonality in the goal-setting process. The goals are then finalized and transferred to a goal-setting planner, and this planner becomes the recorded document for the future measurement of goal achievement. The goals-review process involves both group-goal progress review as well as individual-goal progress review.

The goal-setting and evaluation process is elaborately and religiously adhered to throughout the year. It is believed that there is a direct relationship between setting goals, measuring goal achievement, and quality of patient care (end result variables). If goals are accomplished, then end result variables will also be accomplished.

Needless to say, considerable effort goes into helping managers think about themselves and the process of changing the way they approach goal-setting with their employees. The section at the end of this chapter provides a complete set of the materials used in helping the hospital's managers integrate goal-driven management into their management approach.

Although many management experts and authorities on goal-driven management and OD would argue that these two management philosophies are inconsistent, they are both very much related to organizational improvement, and therefore, cannot be separated.

Note

1. These definitions are found in: Richard Beckhart, *Organization Development, Strategies, and Models* (Reading, Mass.: Addison-Wesley, 1969); hand-outs prepared for a N.T.L. Seminar in organization development held in Bethel, Mass. in 1970; Warren C. Bennis, *Organization Development: Its Nature, Origins, and Prospects* (Reading, Mass.: Addison-Wesley, 1969); and Robert R. Blake and Jane S. Manton, *Building a Dynamic Corporation Thought Grid: Organization Development.* (Reading, Mass.: Addison-Wesley, 1969).

Quiz

Developing An Organization

1. Have you successfully implemented strategies which have improved the overall quality of worklife, as well as performance, in your organization?   Yes   No

   Comments:

2. Do you know what OD is, and how it relates to goal-driven management?   Yes   No

   Comments:

3. Do you know all you need to know about   _____ _____
   organizational development?   Yes   No

   Comments:

Appendix 8A
Using a Team Approach to MBO:
Some Theoretical and Practical Aspects

"MBO" is sometimes subsumed under the label "OD," although traditional MBO is significantly different from OD. Some versions of MBO are congruent with OD, however, and these versions are what this paper is about.

MBO has been defined as:

> A managerial process whereby organizational purposes are diagnosed and met by joining superiors and subordinates in the pursuit of mutually agreed upon goals and objectives, which are specific, measurable, time-bound, and joined to an action plan; progress and goal attainment are measured and monitored in appraisal sessions which center on mutually determined, objective standards of performance.[1]

OD has been defined as:

> . . . a long-range effort to improve an organization's problem-solving and renewal processes, particularly through a more effective and collaborative management of organization culture—with special emphasis on the culture of formal work teams—with the assistance of a change agent, or catalyst, and the use of the theory and technology of applied behavioral science, including action research.[2]

The basic characteristics which differentiate OD from other organization improvement strategies are:

1. High emphasis on group and organizational processes—helping the organization to help itself work better
2. Emphasis on work teams (in contrast to individuals) including the "boss"

This material, written by Wendell F. French, is reprinted with permission from the 1980 Proceedings, VIII Annual MBO State of Art Conference, MBO Institute, Bowling Green, Ohio.

3. Emphasis on a collaborative management of work-team culture—what are we doing that's functional/dysfunctional?
4. Attention to the management of the culture of the total organization
5. Attention to the management of system ramifications as the organizational improvement effort unfolds
6. Use of the action research model
7. Use of a facilitator
8. Viewing the effort as an ongoing process

The action research model pervades much of OD. Its basic components are:

1. Data collection from the client system (work groups)
2. Feedback of data to the client system
3. Problem exploration and diagnosis by the client system
4. Action planning by the client system
5. Action
6. Follow-up
7. Rediagnosis

This participative, diagnostic process is used extensively in OD and underlies most of the interventions.

There are some potential deficiencies in both OD and MBO. Some of the potential deficiencies in OD are listed.

1. Paradoxically, OD can be promoted in an autocratic way.
2. OD can become too team-oriented, too participative, or too interpersonal-relations-oriented to the exclusion of other dimensions.
3. Conversely, OD can become too task-oriented, while ignoring process (including interpersonal, team, and intergroup problems).
4. Long-range success requires a commitment to sustaining the change in organization culture. This is very difficult.
5. Gains are easily eroded by turnover in top management.

Similarly, there are some potential deficiencies in traditional MBO.

1. People can feel locked in, overcontrolled.
2. People often feel pressured to set higher and higher objectives.
3. The measurable aspects can get emphasized to the exclusion of the more spontaneous, creative aspects of the job.

4. Interdependency tends to be underemphasized—frequently, MBO doesn't help much with teamwork.

5. MBO doesn't necessarily improve relationships between superiors and subordinates. (Most organizations do not systematically try to find out if relationships are improved or made worse.)

6. Frequently, MBO programs tend to underemphasize personal objectives.

7. Frequently, performance review doesn't take into account the total situation.

8. MBO can be highly autocratic.

9. MBO can reinforce a one-on-one leadership style (or a team leadership style).

Some of the potential deficiencies of OD can be avoided by systematic data gathering. Some of the potential deficiencies of MBO can be avoided by focusing on intact work teams and emphasizing collaborative problem solving.

I believe that a form of MBO can be designed to capitalize on the diagnostic and participative aspects of OD and to reinforce a team leadership style. A feature of this approach is a broad diagnosis of organizational strengths and problems, and a decision about the relevance of the approach under current circumstances. That form of MBO, which would look something like figure 8A–1, we have called, "Collaborative Management by Objectives"[3] (CMBO),[4] and Rensis Likert has called, "Management by Group Objectives" (MBGO).[5]

Obviously, there are some ingredients that need to be present to make CMBO work. The main ingredient is that the top management group, in particular, must view itself as an effective team and cooperate and help each other. Another important ingredient is that skills in interpersonal communications and group processes must be high enough to permit success. Good intentions but low skills can result in destructive feedback. High skills but intentions to maximize one's own gain at the expense of others will sabotage a team effort.

In particular, these attitudes and skills are needed when individuals of intact teams—with peers and the boss present—review their tentative objectives and when there is a review of the extent to which objectives are accomplished. A problem-solving, supportive mode must be present, or the approach could be destructive instead of constructive. There has been little research on this approach, and little description of this approach in practice. Yet suggestions as to the viability of this approach go back to at least 1967 when Rensis Likert wrote about a successful experiment in group goal-setting involving salesmen.[6]

I believe that "there is gold to be mined" by some organizations if they were to use this approach, and I would recommend careful, gradual experi-

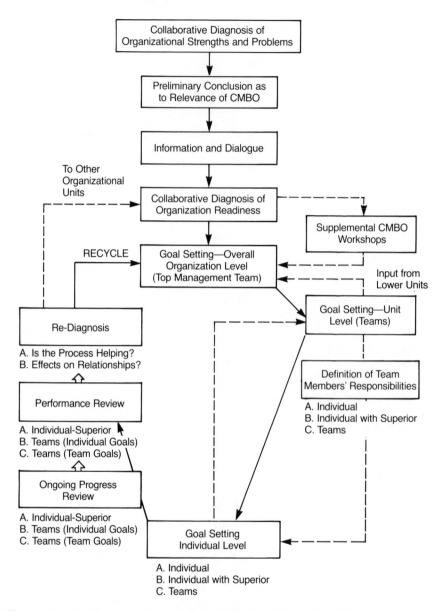

Figure 8A–1. Strategy for Implementing Collaborative Management by Objectives

mentation with some of its features. In some ways, a team approach to MBO may require a kind of built-in, simultaneous OD effort.

Workshop Description

The workshop participants were given this introduction:

This advanced-level workshop will show you how to use a goal-setting model that recognizes the degree of dependency and interdependency needed to accomplish most objectives. You will learn how to differentiate between these two power modes and to be aware of how each is appropriate or inappropriate for effective use of the MBO concept. You will learn how to develop and operationalize an evaluation plan as an integral part of the MBO process.

The following describes the various phases of the workshop in which the participants took part (Phase I to XII).

Phase I

The participants were asked to provide information about: why they attended the session; their expectations of the session; their concerns about the session; their diagnosis of ineffective work groups; and their recommendations for improving the effectiveness of work groups. The participants were asked to evaluate the processes by which they worked in this activity, being aware of the practices which helped and/or hindered the effectiveness of the group.

This activity:

Allowed participants to collect their private thoughts before sharing them with the group

Allowed participants to work in a small group

Allowed participants to practice skills necessary for group goal-setting activities, such as:

Writing (privately, publicly)
Providing ideas (verbally)
Discussing ideas (verbally)
Evaluating products of others

Allowed participants to share pertinent information.

Phase II

The participants were asked to determine the importance of collecting such information prior to doing group work. The experience of the participants during Phase I provided the springboard for this. Since the participants had just been asked to complete a task, they were primed for an evaluation of how well they had performed the task. This provided an immediate opportunity to examine how people live up to what is expected of them.

This activity:

Allowed participants to discover the ingredients of planning activities

Allowed participants to identify a process for monitoring the progress of activities

Allowed participants to identify a process for evaluating activities

Phase III

The participants were introduced to the "human elements" of: truth, my truth, honesty, dishonesty, withholding, and choice. (See Will Schutz's, "Profound Simplicity.")

This activity:

Allowed participants to discover "healthy" concepts to adhere to in living (and working)

Allowed participants the opportunity to choose to conduct their goal-setting activities within what would be a "healthy" climate

Phase IV

The participants were introduced to the concept of "awareness," applying senses and intuition to determine the appropriate actions to take.

This activity:

Allowed participants to discover how to use themselves as the main source of support

Allowed participants to discover how to identify the contribution of their personal goals to group goals (that is, goals of the work session)

Phase V

The participants were introduced to the concept of "straight talk and behavior," using speaking and behaving to get what they want.
   This activity:

   Allowed participants to discover how to communicate more effectively

   Allowed participants to discover how to increase the likelihood of getting what they want

Phase VI

The participants were asked to define the following terms: responsibilities, roles, and relationships. They were then asked to examine how these concepts were related.
   This activity:

   Allowed participants to differentiate between concept and relationships, and between the behavior consistent with these

Phase VII

The participants were introduced to the goal-setting format: goal statements, methods specifications, time specifications, resources (human/material), and questions for evaluation (performance/opinion).
   This activity:

   Allowed participants to learn a format in which their ideas fit and could be documented

   Allowed participants to learn about the relationships between the elements of the format and how these elements contribute to getting what is wanted

   Allowed participants to learn how to use a format to instigate participation to achieve goals

Phase VIII

The participants were introduced to the goal-setting process in individual work and group work.
   This activity:

Allowed participants to determine the appropriate degree and type of participation needed to achieve goals

Allowed participants to determine the appropriate type of support needed to promote participation

Phase IX

The participants were introduced to a method of using the goal-setting format and process in developing an evaluation plan.
This activity:

Allowed participants to discover how the format and process contribute to:

Mission development
Planning
Scheduling
Budgeting
Evaluating

Phase X

The participants were introduced to the relationship between goal-setting format and the degree and type of dependency and interdependency of people and organizational units in setting goals.
This activity:

Allowed participants to identify the necessity of determining the type of support needed from people in order to achieve goals

Allowed participants to identify the relationship of philosophy and psychology on dependency and interdependency

Phase XI

The participants were asked to discuss areas in which the goal-setting format and process could be used in work situations.
This activity:

Allowed participants to test their understanding and comprehension of the concepts which were introduced

Allowed participants to discover how to extrapolate ideas from the format and process and apply them to other situations

Phase XII

The participants were asked to evaluate the activities of the work session and their participation in them.
  This activity:

Allowed participants to determine the productivity of the work session, by using:

  Different evaluation methods
  Different sources of information

Allowed participants to discover how to use information for decision making.

Some Uses of the Goals

1. Orientation
2. Teambuilding
3. Budget planning
4. Financial planning
5. Manpower planning
6. Strategic planning
7. Performance planning
8. Performance review
9. Facilities planning
10. Negotiation for resources
11. Documentation of activities
12. Reviewing activities
13. Scheduling
14. Diagnosis
15. Time management

Notes

1. Mark L. McConkie, "A Clarification of the Goal Setting and Appraisal Processes in MBO." *Academy of Management Review.* vol. 4, no. 1 (1979), pp. 29–40.
2. Wendell L. French and Cecil H. Bell, Jr., *Organization Development* (Englewood Cliffs, NJ: Prentice-Hall, 1978) p. 14.
3. Wendell L. French and Robert W. Hollman, "Management by Objectives: The Team Approach," *California Management Review,* vol. 17, no. 3 (1975), pp. 13–22.
4. Australians suggested that I call this "CoMBO."
5. Renesis Likert and M. Scott Fisher, "MBGO: Putting Some Team Spirit into MBO," *Personnel,* vol. 54, no. 1 (1977), pp. 40–47.
6. Renesis Likert, *The Human Organization* (New York: McGraw-Hill, 1967), pp. 57–59.

Appendix 8B
Sample Materials for Managers Attempting Goal-Driven Management (MBO)

Management Philosophy

Communication

Accurate, clear, and concise information flows horizontally (between and within work groups), as well as vertically (between workers, supervisors and top management).

Decision-Making Practices

Decision-making is participative and takes place at the levels within the organization with the most accurate and complete information (that is, it is decentralized).

Motivational Conditions

The organization encourages, acknowledges, and rewards high levels of employee performance both formally (with promotions and pay increases) and informally (with praise from supervisors). The reinforcement develops a climate of self-motivation by desire, not fear.

Technology Facilities

The hospital uses state-of-the-art, well-maintained and/or efficient equipment, resources, and procedures that meet the needs of the community.

Criteria for an Effective Organization

Each statement describes a work group when it is operative with participative management.

_____ 1. There will be ample, open, candid communications—formal and informal, both vertical and horizontal.

_____ 2. There will be "reality-centered" leadership, a management style appropriate to the reality of the situation.

_____ (3.) Goals, targets, and objectives will be made explicit to everyone in the organization, and progress of these will be reviewed regularly.

_____ 4. Areas of responsibility for each individual will be well defined.

_____ 5. Work will be systematic and well organized, not haphazard and intuitive. Procedures, policies, rules, regulations, and other controls will be minimized, and where they exist will be determined by collaboration and participation.

_____ (6.) Everyone will participate in setting goals and standards of performance, decision-making, establishing controls, planning, setting up of procedures, defining responsibilities, etc.

_____ (7.) Every effort will be made to integrate what the individual wants with what the organization needs, so both the individual and organization accomplish their goals.

_____ 8. There will be a continuous effort to foster creativity at all levels.

_____ 9. There will be a heavy emphasis on learning and the growth and development of individuals. There will be a serious effort to help people maximize their potential.

_____ 10. The climate of the organization, although systematic and orderly, will be flexible and adapt to change.

_____ (11.) Independence, autonomy, and self-control will be stressed, but individuals will be held accountable for the attainment of organizational goals.

_____ 12. The worth of the individual will be stressed, and team relationships will be characterized by a high degree of trust and interdependence. Individuals will be responsible for their own behavior.

_____ 13. Reward and recognition systems will be fair and equitable and will closely relate to actual performance.

_____ 14. Group cooperation and teambuilding will be stressed, and people will have small group loyalties that are integrated with the larger ends and purposes of the total organization.

_____ 15. There will be freedom to experiment, to make mistakes, and to try out new methods—within the overall orderly, systematic effort.

_____ 16. Management systems will be developed through collaboration and participation, and people using the systems will understand them and will feel they can change them when the systems are not working or need improvement.

Hospital Goal Areas

1. Employee Health Services
   Established

2. Religious Services

   TV services—Lenten Service, Easter, Thanksgiving, Christmas, 25th Anniversary Mass, Fr. Burns' Mass
   Special Services

3. Medical Staff Development
   Physician recruitment, e.g., Psychiatry

4. Cost Effectiveness
   Material to Blue Cross Task Force
   CAP Program

5. Education Programs
   Medical Morals
   Patient Education
   CCTV
   Catalogue programs

6. Organization Structure
   ReOrg '79, structure in place

7. Psychiatry Programs
   Preliminary discussions on long-range plans, programs, and facilities
   Renovations started

8. Strategic Planning
   Renovation/additions
   Ambulatory sites
   Chi Systems—long-range plan updated

Criteria for a Good Goal

You must be able to control the outcome.

You must be able to exceed the goal.

You must be able to measure goal achievement.

You must have a monitoring system.

You must be flexible.

Suggested Steps in Group Goal-Setting

Step 1. Discuss purpose of session.

Step 2. Review hospital goals (1979)
         Review 1978 goals/achievement
         Review E.R.V.'s (end result variables).

Step 3. Brainstorm about things that can be done during 1979 to help achieve hospital goals and improve E.R.V.'s.

Step 4. Select 2–3 goals that the group agrees to work on.

Step 5. Write goal in quantitative/specific form (see criteria for good goal).

Step 6. Assign/accept responsibility for working on goal.

Step 7. Review and agree on future action steps.

Suggested Steps in Goal Progress Review

Note: Department members will be meeting with a member of the administrative staff to review goal progress during 1979; this will be done three times as follows: April, July, and year end/January.

Step 1. Review all 1979 goals and assign responsibilities.

Step 2. Review progress towards 1979 goals (the extent to which goals have been or are being achieved).

Step 3. Discuss problems in achieving goals and prepare revised plans for goals if necessary.

Step 4. Review meeting and plans. Discuss further actions.

Quarterly Performance Review
(End Result Variables from O.D. Model)

2nd Quarter   April, May & June

	1977 2nd Qtr.	1977 1st Qtr.	1976 4th Qtr.	1976 3rd Qtr.
Patient Orientation				
Total patients admitted	3,383	3,426	3,293	3,231
Average daily census (adults & children)	286	289	280	263
Average percent of bed occupancy	83.6%	87.4%	81.8%	80.4%
Average length of patient stay	8.1	8.2	8.3	7.9
Average total cost per in-patient day	$189.59	$183.08	$180.50	$177.70
Hours per patient day	16.52	16.19	17.17	16.94
Percentage of re-hospitalization (3 mo.)	N/A	N/A	N/A	N/A
Infection rate—Hospital acquired	2.1%	2.5%	3.0%	1% approx.
Mortality rate	1.7%	1.8%	1.1%	1.8%
Average patient wait in emergency room	N/A	N/A	N/A	N/A
Total number of patient complaints	N/A	11	30	9
Patient's attitude toward hospital	No survey	Good-Ex.	Good-Ex.	Pt. Survey
Medical Staff Orientation				
Total number of medical staff	305	303	298	294
Total number of specialties covered	32	32	31	33
Total number of board certified med. staff	155		155	151
Number of new physicians recruited	7	7	11	25
Number of physicians leaving	1	0	7	6
Consultation rate	45.0%	40.1%	42.2%	41.6%
Number of complaints by medical staff to hospital	2	2	N/A	N/A
Employee Orientation				
Total employment	1,248	1,191	1,178	1,170
Employee turnover	10.8%	12.8%	14.9%	23.0%
Number of requisitions received	100	82	90	110
Amount of requisition lag time	NS = 8 G = 4	NS = 12 G = 19	NS = 17 G = 11	Pending
Number of internal promotions	51	17	20	19
Number of suspensions	N/A	N/A	N/A	Pending
Percentage of sick pay/total regular hrs.	2.2%	2.4%	2.0%	1.7%
Number of overtime/total regular hrs.	1.6%	1.9%	1.9%	1.5%
Number of cont. educ. programs offered	27	16		
Total attendance at cont. educ. programs	676	598		
Employee attitude toward hospital				Survey
Organization Orientation				
Optimal percentile on H.A.S.	N/A	3.4%	3.5%	3.3%
Budgeted revenue Y.T.D.	6.2% O	5.9% O	1.6% O	1.3% U
Budgeted expense Y.T.D.	2.0% U	1.5% U	0.1% U	2.2% U
Budgeted payroll expense Y.T.D.	5.0% U	5.1% U	5.0% U	6.7% U
Net profit percent of revenue Y.T.D.	11.9%	16.3%	5.1%	5.0%

9
Team Building and Performance Improvement

Our forces are one team in the game to win regardless of who carries the ball. This is no time for "fancy dans" who won't hit the line with all they have on every play, unless they can call the signals. Each player on the team—whether he shines in the spotlight of the backfield or eats dirt in the line—must be an All-American.
—Omar Bradley

A medium-sized plant of a large midwestern corporation was ranked next to last in both quality and profitability when compared to the corporation's other plants. Initially, the plant manager felt that the problem was due to ineptness of supervisors in managing their staff and that if this could be corrected the plant would become profitable and quality would improve. After careful analysis through observation, interviews and other processes, it was concluded that three factors contributed to the plant's poor performance. First, managers acted and made decisions in an independent and isolated way, showing little or no concern for one another. Second, managers conducted their work in a manner that was counterproductive to other members of the management team. Third, interpersonal relationships among members of the management team were depressingly crude.

It was decided that a team-building approach would be used to work with these problems. Initially, the process started out as an interpersonal confrontation. This led to role clarification and redefinition, and finally to development of interdependent and supportive relationships. The effect of careful analysis and a step-by-step team-building approach led the plant to improve its ranking in the corporation from second from the bottom to second from the top, with a 20 percent improvement in quality and a profitability increase from $75,000 loss per month to approximately the same profit per month.

From this experience one can conclude that it is quite unlikely that the problem would have been solved if the original hasty diagnosis had been carried out. The important message in this example is the **need for analysis and careful consideration of the starting point for team building.** Team building is not a panacea for all organization problems, as some would lead you to believe. In fact, team building, conceived as interpersonal confrontation only, may be totally wrong as a means to solve organizational problems.

For purposes of our discussion, a team is a group of people who must work in an interdependent way with regard to setting goals, making plans, achieving plans, and communicating problems to accomplish their jobs.[1] Expressing this in another way, the effective team may require a session of "team building" when it is not solving its problems or reasonably achieving existing goals. Some of the typical symptoms a work unit will notice when they are not working well together include: loss of production, increased complaints, indecisiveness, apathy, lack of initiative and innovation, poor meetings, high dependency on the boss, and continued unaccounted increases in costs.[2]

An analysis of any problem that involves managers will necessarily encompass a variety of contributing factors; that is, the analysis is multivariant. For instance, the typical factors that need to be considered include an understanding of individual needs, a clarification of job roles, a knowledge of the resource requirements for the team to perform effectively, an understanding of the relationships between team members, and a study of the procedures and practices that the team is required to follow. It would be inappropriate, for example, to hold an interpersonal team-building session when the relationships between team members are satisfactory and the problem actually rests in a set of improperly designed procedures or practices; or it might be inappropriate to conduct a team-building session for the purpose of setting goals or defining a mission when the real problem is how people are working together.

It is important to develop a rationale for diagnosis and analysis prior to the actual practice of team building. We will, therefore, look at the factors relating to effective performance when a team building intervention would be appropriate to solve or correct situations contributing to inadequate performance.

Contributing Factors

For clarification, let us define each of the major contributing factors that affect performance and are related to team effectiveness. First, it is important to conceptualize the team as a group of managers who work together on a day-to-day basis, and where the relationships between these managers is *interdependent*. That is to say, what one manager does affects the output and quality of work of another. In essence, a management team cannot perform effectively if individual managers perform as if in a vacuum.

Individual Needs. Individual needs are defined as the personal characteristics and underlying drives that each member of the management team possesses. Individual needs reflect personal beliefs and values, intellectual abilities, interests, and a host of personality characteristics. These drives and underlying characteristics serve to motivate the individual and in turn direct him/her to accomplish tasks, goals, and activities. Often one person's drives contradict another's. Often, this will show up in the work environment in a very simple form. For example, one manager prefers to discuss problems with other managers in order to test ideas, while another manager prefers to work on his/her own. You can see the problem that could be created when these two managers might attempt to work together.

Role Definition. Often the problem with teams is due to unclear roles and responsibilities of members. When these definitions are not clear, managers frequently seek to promote their own interests and create responsibilities for themselves that have not, in fact, been authorized by the organization or recognized by other members of the team, causing overlapping and misunderstanding, not to mention open conflict.

Resources. When organizations set goals, they often fail to give the management team the resources needed to achieve the goals. In the example cited above, the plant was old and the organization had decided not to make any large capital investments. Thus, it was extremely difficult for the management team, under the best of conditions, to achieve its goals.

Relationships. People work together in a cause-effect manner. Relationships are unique in that many of their workings, in the form of behavior, are visible to people in the organization. Relationships, because they involve behavior, can be changed, whereas intellect, values, beliefs, and other personal needs are much more difficult to change. Therefore, the relationship area provides opportunities for team improvement that may not be present when dealing with individual needs.

Procedures and Practices. Organizations may sometimes impose procedures and practices on management teams that lead to conflict. For example, one department may be required to audit another department, which can lead to suspicion and distrust. Or sometimes a procedure introduced at a higher level in the organization will actually contradict or duplicate a procedure already in existence within another department. These contradictions, conflicts, and duplications lead to fall-outs and open fights among the management team, with each manager trying to serve his own department as opposed to working towards a common goal.

The reason for listing the above definitions is to provide a framework for initial data collection, which will eventually lead to decisions regarding what approach should be used in team building.

Approaches to Team Development

There are a variety of well-described and widely practiced approaches used in team development. Many times the approach used is a result of a very brief and cursory exploration of the *need* for team building. For example, one internal consultant classifies his/her organization's team building approach as: "Focusing on role issues, procedural issues, and interpersonal issues."[3]

Obviously these approaches deal with some of the factors that we discussed previously. The difficulty, however, is that the analysis and decision regarding the correct approach is often overlooked. Instead, the approach chosen is a result of the whims, fancies, and abilities of the consultant to sell a particular idea.

Another approach to classification of team development activities examines the circumstances when the need for team building may be highest. For example, team building may be needed when a new team is formed, when the performance of an existing team requires improvement, or when unhealthy counterproductive agreements need to be overcome. Again, the approach involves looking at the entire situation, as opposed to looking at only the specific factors causing ineffective or effective team work. Clearly, team builders fall prey to only impressions, and to opportunities for prescribing cures which are easily labeled and therefore accepted by management. It is far more difficult to say, "I don't know, but I do know how to study and analyze in order to pinpoint cause and effect." If out of searching grows team building, so be it.

One further classification includes:

The Future: goal setting and planning to meet goals

Team Processes: procedures for meeting and communicating

Interfaces with the Environment: demands placed by the environment[4]

This classification sorts out the sources or focuses that the team building process should look into, but does not look at the factors which contribute to the ability of the team to perform.

We propose to design team-building strategies on the basis of careful analysis of factors that underlie the way in which the team works. This includes an examination of individual needs, role definitions, resources, relationships, procedures, and practices.

An Analysis Model

In order to develop the appropriate strategy for team building, it is essential to carefully analyze each of the factors leading to the ability of the team to work together effectively. As previously defined, these factors would fit into the model in figure 9–1. This model resembles the general intervention steps in a typical organization development project. When a problem flares up in any of the areas of role definitions, relationships, etcetera, this problem should be viewed first as a symptom of a possible greater ill. Analysis of each of the symptoms should develop an awareness and understanding of the greater ill, which in turn should lead to the design of a team-development strategy which would attack not merely the symptoms, but the heart of the greater ill; and by curing the greater ill, the symptoms are reduced. It is important to note that the strategy does not "lock in" on one factor, but approaches the team development activity as a series of substrategies, each requiring different tactics or intervention approaches.

Figure 9–1. Flow in Team-Building Process

Suppose you were asked to work with a group of managers, and in your initial contact with the president of the company, he/she expressed concern about the way managers were working together. He/she cited examples of extensive disagreement, difficulties in arriving at decisions, "back biting," undermining, and a variety of other things. Initially, these symptoms would imply the need for some form of interpersonal team building activity.

However, an analysis of the situation revealed several things. The organization had ample resources from its parent organization, but the procedures that managers were following were ill-defined, since the organization had only recently divested from one corporation and had been acquired by another. Relationships, then, were indeed a major problem. Roles and job responsibilities were inadequately defined and misunderstood. And finally, there were personal differences among team members, including nationality differences (two members were from the Orient, one from Argentina, one from England, and the others from a variety of backgrounds in the United States).

The analysis of this case suggests that many of the relationship problems were caused by unclear role definitions, coupled with personal differences caused by dissimilar cultural backgrounds. The greater ill is clearly not the resources being provided, and probably has little to do with the procedures and practices. As a result of analysis, you would ask the president to put together a team building activity aimed at improving interpersonal relationships.

The most obvious point from which to start team building involves role definition. As roles are clarified, individuals reveal their feelings and their differences in personal needs, which ultimately leads to the enrichment of the interpersonal aspects of the team. Interestingly enough, following the clarification of roles and the awareness of personal differences, the relationships question becomes less critical.

It is generally believed that team building basically involves interpersonal exploration and confrontation. Interpersonal relationships may be a cause or a manifestation of a variety of other kinds of problems, including lack of resources, inadequate procedures and practices, poor role definition, and differences in individual needs. All practitioners should carefully analyze factors involved in poor team performance at the onset of team building. As a result of this analysis, the practitioner can then design the strategy for team development that will approach the problem at its most sensitive point, moving from this point to those factors that are a direct outgrowth of the heart of the problem. Following this process, it is quite likely and probable that successful team building will be the result.

Notes

1. This definition was originated by Jack McMahon, Johnson Wax Company, Racine, Wisconsin.

2. Glenn H. Varney and Ronald Hunady, "Team Building and Individual Change," *ASTD Report #2*, Madison, Wisconsin, 1978.

3. McMahon, Johnson Wax Company.

4. Source unknown.

Quiz

Team Building and Performance Improvement

1. Is there complete teamwork among those working for you?

    Yes   No

2. Do members of your work group work together in a   _____   _____
    cooperative and supportive way?   Yes   No

3. Is the trust level as high as it could be in your work   _____   _____
    group?   Yes   No

4. Is the output of your work group as high as it   _____   _____
    should be?   Yes   No

10
Coordinating Managerial Excellence

> Order is not pressure which is imposed from without but an equilibrium which is set up from within.
>
> ——José Oretega y Gasset

Very little has been written about how to internally administer and manage organizational improvement. However, one individual, Dr. Gene Seyna of the Eastman Kodak Company, has thoroughly researched the process of coordinating goal-oriented, management change, and he has studied, in particular, the role of a Goal-Driven Management coordinator.* According to Dr. Seyna, two basic factors are necessary for a successful change to goal-oriented management: management must participate in the administration of the program, and a "first-rate coordinator," someone who has the full responsibility of moving organizational improvement along, is needed.

It is easy to see how the role of the goal-driven management coordinator can be confused. In a study conducted by Dr. Seyna, it was found that the people responsible for coordinating goal-oriented programs were cast into a variety of jobs. A sample list of the types of titles and the percentage of time devoted to goal-driven management is in table 10–1.

An examination of this list raises questions concerning what actually has to be done to successfully shift an organization to a goal-driven approach. In recent years, goal-oriented management has evolved into a process of managing that relates directly to the organization's philosophy and manner of operation. An effective change-program usually emphasizes goal-driven management instead of just setting goals (see the hospital example in Appendix 8A). It also emphasizes a certain way of thinking in which:

1. The goal-setting process is only a small part of the overall management philosophy.
2. Thinking and flexibility are required.

---

*Dr. Seyna is past President of the MBO Institute, Bowling Green, Ohio. Much of the material presented in this chapter is taken directly from his work.

Table 10–1
Titles Used for Coordinators of Management Excellence

Title	Reports to	Percentage of Time Spent on Goal-Driven Management
Administrative Assistant	President, Chairman	5
Director, Planning & Evaluation	Director of Administrative Services	20
Asst. VP, Executive	Chairman and CEO	15
Manager, Distribution Development & Quality Assurance	Manager, Distribution Engineer, VP–Distribution (MBO)	10
Administrative Officer III	Program Adminsitrator I	75
MBO/R Program Manager	General in Command, Management Div.	75
Performance Assurance Spec.	Manager, Performance Assurance	50
Manager, Training & Employee Development	Director Employee Relations	35
Manager of Corporate Objectives	Director, Special Services	90
Branch Manager, Special Activities Director	Assistant Executive Director	80
Vice President, Manufacturing	President	10
MBO Coordinator, Director Special Prog. Evaluation		10–15
Vice President, Corporate Planning	President	50
Executive Director	Board of Directors	20
Director, Results Management	Vice-President of Division	100
Results Management Coordinator	Manager of Division	100
Manager, Manufacturing	President	10
Director, Management Objectives	Vice-President, Planning	100
Industrial Relations Mgr.	General Manager	10
Director of Employee Education	Associate Administrator (Hospital)	10–90
Controller, Service Div.	General Manager	5
Executive Vice President	Board of Directors	15
Manager, Industrial	Vice-President, Manufacturing Group	80
Group Personnel Consultant	Managing Director	40
Director of OD	Executive Officer, Personnel & Labor Rel.	60
Coordinator of Organization and Staff Development	Director of Personnel	20
Manager, Administrative Services	Vice-President, Inform. Systems	40
Training and Safety Director	Vice-President, Personnel	40
Coordinator, Information Systems	Director, Administration and Analysis	25

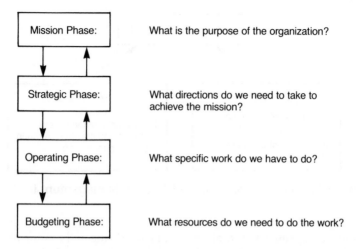

Figure 10–1. Four Phases of Goal-Oriented Management in KODAK

3. All management processes involve thinking along goal-driven management lines.

4. The entire organization needs to interact on a goal-driven management basis.

5. Goals grow out of the organization's mission statements.

6. Goal-driven management is a long-term program.

7. Detailed planning is included in addition to the budgeting process.

8. Behavioral change is required on the part of all management.

According to Dr. Seyna, the goal-oriented management he uses in the Eastman Kodak Company is separated into four phases (see figure 10–1).

According to Seyna, "when we describe the goal-oriented managing process to a manager who is interested in starting this concept of managing, the following checklist can show him/her the major areas which need to be developed in a long-term effort with each group in his/her organization." This list includes:

Prepare a mission statement

List key result-areas

Analyze the strengths, weaknesses, opportunities, and threats

Develop strategic plans

Produce group goals

Prepare individual position-guides

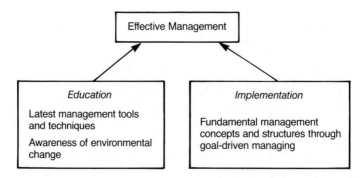

Figure 10–2. Two Contributors to Effective Management in KODAK

Produce individual action-plans—problem-solving and routine objectives

Prepare personal goals

Develop continuing educational and skills-improvement programs

Install and utilize the needed information systems

Develop a coordinated performance-evaluation-and-reward system

Learn to budget for priorities

Set up review and control systems

To summarize, Seyna states that the objective is to achieve "more effective management." To do this, two broad approaches are utilized: education—to develop the necessary good practices of management; and implementation—to assure that these practices are carried out (see figure 10–2).

The Role of a Coordinator of Managerial Excellence

How many hats does a coordinator have to wear? Overall, the coordinator must have many talents; the coordinator must act as a trainer, pusher, facilitator, advisor, catalyst, organizer, administrator, referee, analyst, evangelist, coach, politician, teamwork-builder, motivator, and the list goes on. The important point is that the coordinator's task is to change the total organization from one form of managing to another, and this task requires a multiplicity of skills. Specifically, Dr. Seyna lists the personal attributes that one of his coordinators wrote down (with tongue in cheek) as being absolutely necessary for successful installation and coordination of change.

Coordinator Attributes

Attributes Absolutely Necessary

Be sensitive to the organization's climate; sense when to push harder or pull back.

Get a reasonable amount of respect from management for your abilities, whatever they are. (Preferably, the coordinator has had some practical experience in that company.)

Get support from top management, plus the immediate superior. When the coordinator says something, everyone knows on whose behalf it is said.

Move around and be visible. Don't be an introvert.

Be flexible. Adjust your personality to fit the audience. For example, be flamboyant with a customer-outlook for marketing, hard-nosed with manufacturing.

Let the credit for your achievements go to those who implement them, yet, to some extent, accept the blame when implementation fails.

Convince others that your ideas are really theirs, and then help to implement them.

Resist frustration which will certainly occur. Get a "sounding board" to voice your frustrations and vent feelings—this helps ease the tension.

Be *positive* when talking about change to others.

Be dynamic and enthusiastic about the job. (Obviously, the coordinator must believe in it absolutely.)

Never accept a status-quo situation; never accept traditional methods; question everything (but don't be a bottleneck); and be absolutely unafraid to differ with your superiors and peers if you believe otherwise.

Be able to "read" people—their real motives may be different from what they say.

Understand the complexity of the total management process, and the real (versus textbook) role of the manager.

Be very flexible when implementing change. Have a focused end result always in mind, but vary the approach, if necessary to keep on course for that end result.

Never believe you can establish rigid procedures for change.

Be faster than a speeding bullet, more powerful than a locomotive, able to leap tall buildings in a single bound (the Superman claim).

Helpful (But Not Necessary) Attributes

Don't be academic—especially to hard-nosed old-timers.

Have a well-rounded education and experience-base to understand the total role of management, and to quickly see the forest from the trees when confronted by the "specialist."

Don't be an empire builder.

Use outside consultants, when necessary, to keep the approach "sparking," but don't be overwhelmed by their approach.

Have the ear of the CEO. This gives the coordinator a better feel for the company and current problems.

Be an entertaining presenter.

Think strategically, and be a good planner—pay attention to detail.

What a Coordinator Really Does

Calls meetings to explain and update the goal-oriented approach

Acts as a catalyst for change by introducing management audits, "think tanks", etcetera

Introduces goal-directed concepts into the management (and planning) cycle of the company, including concepts such as: appraisal, salary administration, strategic planning, management development, manpower planning, general management meetings, and projects

Teaches: in classroom lectures and open discussions, by circulating articles and books, by writing refresher memos on goals, objective status, and plans, and in formal training courses

Reviews both objectives and plans, when requested by others, for effectiveness, style, methodology, and coordination and communication gaps

Helps develop agendas for various seminars and meetings, to give them the proper focus

Walks on water . . . ice, snow!!

A Task Force to Install Goal-Driven Management

A task force is always utilized to implement goal-driven management; the coordinator is the chairman of the task force, which usually reports formally, sometimes informally, to the change coordinator. Generally, the tasks which are to be accomplished by such a group include:

1. Act as a management consulting group and develop the goal-directed system that is best suited to the organization.
2. Produce a plan for the introduction of goal setting and then assist with the implementation.
3. Act as spokesman for the unit they represent and assure that their unit is moving at the same speed and in the same direction as the other units.

4. Act as teachers, consultants, and guides for their unit's management and personnel.

Problems Frequently Encountered by the Goal-Driven Management Coordinator

Dr. Senya cites a variety of different problems that MBO coordinators face. Several of these are cited.

> *Being sandbagged.* This means getting promises from managers who say they are enthusiastic and will support the effort. Sometimes such support means sitting back and giving a benevolent nod of the head. Active and steady participation must be given by the top manager and his immediate subordinates; they must set the lead.
>
> *Flying blind.* Top management may be actively participating in reviewing everyone else's objectives, but may be refusing to develop the organization mission statement and strategic objectives. Without this overall direction, subordinates will not know which objectives to set—leading to organizational ineffectiveness and cynicism on the part of those subordinates who do write objectives.
>
> *Itchy pants.* It is often difficult for the coordinator to get a management group away from the office to spend a day or two on SWOT—analysis of strengths, weaknesses, opportunities, and threats—and strategic planning. Many managers feel guilty about not being at their desks working. They are caught in George Odiorne's "activity trap": being busy is work, thinking is not. The coordinator has to be patient and convince managers that their subordinates expect these plans. Since this is also an educational process, the coordinator should get managers to read the important articles and texts on management and planning.
>
> *Magic solutions.* No matter how careful the coordinator is in explaining that there are no secrets to goal-oriented management, some managers will keep looking for magic. They cannot believe that goal-oriented management is simply organized common sense coupled with a firmly declared resolve to keep commitments. The coordinator should take plenty of time when introducing goal-oriented management to uninitiated managers, to allow everyone an opportunity to digest all that is presented and to ask questions. I have found that a discussion of the evolution of management will clearly demonstrate that goal-oriented management is neither a fad nor a panacea but is solidly based on all prior management experience.

Basic foundation. If a goal-oriented management program is to be successful, a certain amount of basic professional knowledge is needed by all participants: management theory, planning processes, motivation, group interactions, up-to-date skills in jobs, environmental monitoring, marketing, etcetera. Not everyone needs an MBA degree, but a basic foundation of knowledge is necessary for people to really understand what they are trying to accomplish and why. Expensive outside programs and seminars are not needed; the coordinator should develop a reading list of articles and texts, and set up group discussion for appropriate films and tapes.

Chinese walls. No matter what kind of an organization the coordinator works in, there are walls, suspicions, and antagonisms between groups. For example, financial people are certain that sales people have an easy life and spend a lot of the company's money on fun, while they themselves have to sit at their desks and save money; sales people, on the other hand, complain that the narrow-minded, penny-pinching, financial staff prevents them from making more sales. It's only human nature to band together with your own and be suspicious of all others. A way to overcome this problem, when developing a goal-oriented management program, is to set up a task force that includes a representative from each group. This really works miracles in developing good teamwork across groups, since each representative is reporting back to his/her people on progress and the need for coordination. Each group then feels it is part of the development.

Strategic planning. Strategic planning has come to be an exciting process that most people feel is their job. Actually, everyone does a bit of strategic planning, but the proportion varies considerably depending upon the level of the individual. A chief executive may spend 50–60% of his/her time on long-range planning, while a low-level supervisor might devote only a few hours a year. The coordinator sorts this out so that the bottom levels are devoting their efforts to accomplishing operational objectives.

Quantification. Some people will spend most of the time worrying and arguing about how to quantify every objective completely and accurately. Sometimes these arguments will become fierce and can divert everyone away from the true question: "Is this the objective we should be striving for?" "Is this the best way to do it?" "Who should be involved?" "Why are we doing it?"

"What are they trying to do to me now?" If goal-oriented management is introduced too fast for people to ask questions, adapt, and become comfortable, employees will become suspicious and believe that goal-

driven management is a new scheme to harm them. Time must be given for change to occur gradually, with the opportunity for all questions to be answered.

We cannot cover all the potential problems in this section. Some other objections a coordinator might meet, plus suggested solutions, are:

Lack of management interest. Don't begin without management interest; if you have to, try education, and pressure from lower levels.

No follow-up on objectives. Set up a regular review-cycle, perhaps once a quarter.

Psychological fears and barriers. Use a slow introduction, with education and much individual coaching.

Poor supervision. Educate concerning the role of the supervisor.

Poor horizontal communication. Force communication by requiring all groups concerned to discuss the development of an objective.

Too much paperwork. The only documents really needed are the written objective and position guide; let any other documents be used as desired by the people.

Unrealistic expectations. Avoid a "circus" introduction filled with promises of magic solutions.

"Not for us." Fight this with education and careful questions that lead the resisters to recognize that goal-oriented management is what they are already trying to do, but so far without much success.

The task of implementing and moving a change program through an organization requires the attention of skilled and talented people. There are no magic solutions for the coordinator of change. It takes patience, perseverence, friendly coaching, and a long time. But the results are well worth the effort.

Self-Assessment of Skills Necessary for Change Coordination

The self-assessment wheel in figure 10–3 is designed to help you think about the skills needed to successfully fill the change coordinator's shoes. It can then be used as a part of the selection process when appointing a change coordinator.

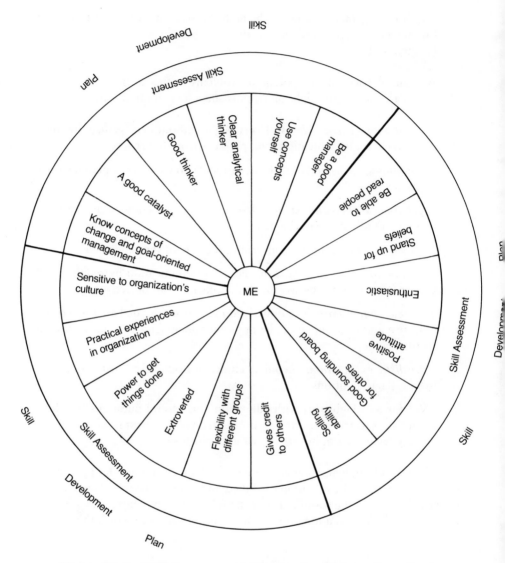

Figure 10–3. Skill Assessment Planner for Change Coordinators

Quiz

Coordinating Managerial Excellence

1. Do you know what you need to know about
    coordinating a goal-driven management program?   Yes   No

    Comments:

2. Do you have a complete list of things you need to
    do to make goal-driven management work?   Yes   No

    Comments:

3. Do you have the goal-driven management program
    reporting to the right person in your organization?   Yes   No

    Comments:

Appendix A
Goal-Driven Management in Different Situations: A Collection of Approaches

I n the early years of goal-driven management, its concepts were applied primarily to line functions in major manufacturing concerns. In the late fifties, a group of chief executive officers met with Larry Apply, then president of the American Management Association (AMA), to study the possibility of applying what the AMA called "standards of performance" as an effective measure of organizational performance. Standard Oil of Ohio, Harris Intertype, and a variety of other companies began to implement programs using standards of performance. As these concepts spread, they eventually became a working philosophy for the management of numerous organizations, and many organizations applied these concepts to all functions of management. At this date, articles and books have been written concerning almost every area where goal-driven management can be applied.

This chapter will provide a sampling of the different types of applications, and in particular, will provide the various types of goals established for various types of functions. At the end of this chapter you will find a listing of publications relating to the application of goal-driven management to different functional areas and different types of organizations.

We have selected several examples to include in this section:

Goals for production managers

Goals for financial managers

Goals for marketing and sales managers

Goals for a variety of other staff positions

These examples are not held up as ideal illustrations but are provided as reference points to help you consider the various applications available to you. Investigate and read to further your understanding of how goal-directed management can be adapted to your situation.

Goals for Production Managers

Chief Industrial Engineer

Major Segments of Position	Standards of Performance (Conditions Which Will Exist When Each Segment is Performed Satisfactorily)
1. Administers and supervises the work and people necessary to provide and apply the best possible industrial engineering practices, job standards, methods, plant layout, work sampling, routing, etc.	A. Incentive coverage is at _____% by Dec. 31, 19 _____. B. Supervisors know how to apply standards, or corrective steps have been taken: training, individual conferences, etcetera C. Operators on incentives average _____% efficiency by Dec. 31, 19 _____. D. Cost reductions resulting directly from applied industrial engineering practices, on an annual basis, are in excess of any increase in the department's operating costs. E. Percent make-up pay to incentive labor will be _____% by Dec. 31, 19 _____. F. New or revised plant layouts will be within budgeted estimates and justified by cost-reduction payoff within three years. G. Routing and machine-loading practices will eliminate scheduling problems and enhance cost reduction. H. Standard practice sheets are accurate and up-to-date. I. Job standards are audited once every two years on a scheduled basis.
2. Supervises and administers the people and the work necessary to provide new and/or improved tooling for manufacturing operations	A. Final results show that cost-reduction or quality-improvement estimates for justification of expense(s) are accurate. B. Tooling produces a product that meets engineering "specs." C. Costs of this company's tooling are less than from other companies: cost data must support this. D. Completion dates on new and/or improved tooling jobs are met and production delays are avoided.
3. Supervises work force necessary to provide efficient tooling maintenance, tool grinding, and tool storage	A. Established product-quality levels directly related to tooling are maintained. B. Planned tooling maintenance program eliminates production delays that might have resulted from defective tooling. C. Operator waiting-time at tool crib is within allowable standards. D. Perishable-tool costs are within budget estimates.

Major Segments of Position	Standards of Performance (Conditions Which Will Exist When Each Segment is Performed Satisfactorily)
	E. Tool-grinding work is up-to-date, and all tools are ground to specifications.
4. Performs and/or supervises all work necessary to provide data relating to the acquisition, replacement, and special maintenance of all plant equipment, tooling, machines, buildings-savings, justification for expenses, costs comparisons, etc.	A. Completed by due date. B. Audits and operating-results prove accuracy.
5. Organizes and plans work for the department	A. Work is planned on an annual basis and completion dates are set for projects— annual written report(s) to general manager. B. Completion dates are met on all projects— monthly reports to general manager. C. Department work is divided to best utilize employees' abilities. D. Employees' assignments and responsibilities are clearly defined.
6. Trains and develops all supervised employees	A. Specific plans are used for training. B. Employees are given added responsibilities as employees are ready. C. Standards of performance are established for each employee and are reviewed (at least) annually and/or when responsibilities are changed. D. Employees meet standards of performance. E. Internal training and/or outside sources are continuously used to keep industrial engineering staff up-to-date on practices, methods, etc.
7. Communicates effectively with superior, staff personnel, subordinates, and others, to maintain efficiency of department	A. Performance of department personnel indicates the employees are being kept informed about company policies, pay, benefits, rules, company plans, etc. Absenteeism is at or below _____%; turnover is at or below _____%. B. Accurate information and correct practices are passed on to supervisors to avoid problems concerning job standards, methods, etc. C. All reports are accurate and submitted by due date. D. Accurate industrial-engineering data for operating decisions is being supplied through staff meetings, manufacturing meetings, and various other meetings.

Manufacturing Engineering

Responsibility	Standard

Finance	A. Meet established 19_____ profit plan budgets:
	    Expense
	    Tooling
	    Capital
	
	B. Meet overall cost-reduction goal of $ _____.
	    Meet M.E. cost-reduction goal of $ _____.
	
	C. Meet operating, cost-equivalent, unit goal of:
	    $ _____ general
	    $ _____ special projects
	    _____
	    $ _____ total
	
	D. Assist manufacturing to meet goal of reducing waste and variable accounts by _____% or more, compared with last year.
	
	E. Assist in reducing overall (automatic) total-labor costs per unit.

Schedules	A. 100% schedule realization.
Hourly Personnel	A. Improve absenteeism performance over last year's average performance. (19_____ average, 3.3%).

Safety	Improve over 19_____ performance.
	
	19_____: Lost time _____
	             Frequency _____
	             Severity _____
	             Medical frequency _____

Labor Relations	Early attention to labor relations problems so they do not develop into major issues: A. Reduce _____% of grievances settled per foreman or superintendent's answer. B. Keep grievances to a minimum. C. Improve foreman's ability to handle day-to-day problems.
Quality	Provide the services needed to meet division goals. Bring new models and engineering changes into production to meet quality goals.
Housekeeping	A. Meet _____% average performance of 19_____, based on improved standards in housekeeping, in accordance with model division objectives.

Responsibility	*Standard*
Facilities, Equipment, Tooling and Processing	Division projects:

1. Total costs and savings, where applicable, to meet the stated objectives for each project established when appropriations were approved. Consideration to be given to the following: degree of risk, design and development requirements, required time schedules, complexity, know-how, and other factors involved.

2. Schedules of projects to be met in accordance with division and group programs.

3. Based on profit-plan schedule, maintenance-cost/ direct-labor dollar is not to exceed _____% average for 19_____.

4. Establish a data-processing scheduling system for maintenance in units.

5. General maintenance cost per unit not to exceed $____ for total year 19_____. Tool maintenance cost per unit goals for 19_____:

Automatic	$_____/unit
Combination	$_____/unit
Oven	$_____/unit

6. Down-time goals for 19_____:

   Tool-failure average is _____% hrs./direct labor hr.

   Machine-failure average is _____% hrs./direct labor hr.

Inventory	
Materials and Handling	Assist in overall unit-program to reduce costs.
	Complete 19_____ warehouse addition.

Management, Development, and Training

A. Increase the number of approved back-up candidates for key positions in manufacturing-engineering.

B. Quality of new employees is more than adequate.

C. Evidence of improved effectiveness of managers on their jobs.

D. 40% of management people show involvement in at least one self-development activity.

Communication

Evidence of improved working relationships between individuals and departments.

Improved relationships between people on same level but in different departments.

Purchasing Agent

Key-Result Area	Measurement Factor	Standard of Performance	Basis of Measurement (F) Factual, (J) Judgment
Delivery of purchased parts within established lead times	Composite short-list by machine	Maintain _____% of all received parts during established lead times for period 8/15 to 1/1.	(F) Every other week, analysis of composite short-list by machine
Improved procedures	Processing of invoices	Devise and install a method for processing invoices that are date-stamped 10 days old or older. _____% of all invoices that are 10 days old or older will be processed on time during period 8/15 to 1/1.	(F) Date stamped on invoice vs. date processed for payment
Analysis of major vendors	Delivery performance	_____% of all parts supplied by these vendors will be received on time by 1/1.	(F) Comparison of dates on follow-up copies of purchase orders
	Quality	_____% of all parts supplied by these vendors meet our quality standards by 1/1.	(F) Weekly rejection-report received from quality control
	Price	Products supplied by these vendors will be priced the same as or lower than competitors by 1/1.	(F) Competitive bidding on periodical basis for all categories
Pricing	Pricing file	To have the _____ account usage and pricing records installed in new pricing file: _____% complete by 10/1.	(F) & (J) Spot check as travelers are typed out
Housekeeping	Neat department	Everything in place by 10/15.	(J) Visual inspection
Accuracy of records	Comparison of travelers in both receiving and raw stock with open orders	Correlation of P.O.'s and travelers 100% accurate by 10/15.	(F) Spot check every other week
Cost reduction	Purchased material	Install and complete a formal cost-reduction program resulting in savings of $50,000 by 1/1.	(F) & (J) Formal reports written that describe action taken and results achieved
Cost improvement	Divisional value-analysis program	Investigate and evaluate the justification for the reestablishment of this division's value-analysis program by 1/1.	(F) Report submitted on time (J) Completeness and quality of report
Quality of products shipped	Machines shipped	After 9/15, no machines shipped that do not meet quality and operating specifications 100%.	(F) Quality assurance in manager's report (check list-report copy shipped with machine) (F) Field service representative's report (check list-report returned with verified copy of quality-assurance manager's report)

Key-Result Area	Measurement Factor	Standard of Performance	Basis of Measurement: (F) Factual, (J) Judgment
			(J) Correlation between 1 2 above (checked by quality-assurance manager and field-sales manager)
			(J) Customer acceptance of machine (develop new-customer acceptance report and procedure)
	Operation of machine during warranty period	Reduce warranty failures after 10/1 by: A. Analysis of failures, by type of machines B. Analysis of failures, by function of machines C. Recommending action to all concerned, to reduce failures. Goal to be ____% for period 10/1 to 1/1.	(F) Number and kind of failures, and seriousness of impact on customer operations (F) Number of failures in relation to statistics compiled and updated periodically
	Quality of attachments (change parts)	All tooling shipped after 10/15 is to function on customer's machines, according to specifications	(F) Number of malfunctions and service reports experienced after 10/15 (J) Number of malfunctions attributable to division activities; development of statistical reporting of external causes, and development of ways to prevent them; verification of proper assembly of machine and of proper adjustments (settings) of machine by field service reports
	Repair parts	Reduce shipment of defective critical-parts to customers by ____% of present level by 10/1.	(F) Number and kind of complaints from customers
	Quality of all inventoried wear parts	Maintain small inspection program for all wear parts inventory to maintain quality of lots at ____%.	(F) Program is complete and statistically sound, program is in effect
	Quality and responsibility consciousness of all division personnel	Assist in development of a plan for a quality-consciousness campaign by 9/1. Prepare for installation of plan by 9/1. Improved employee attitude toward, and heightened knowledge of, quality responsibility by 1/1.	(F) Completeness of plan; approval of plan by general manager; workability and reasonability of costs (F) Plan is ready and actually put into effect. Smoothness of: spot checks and interviews (F) & (J) Personal interviews; visits to plant areas by department heads; project accomplishment

Plant Manager

	Standard	Performance		
		First Quarter	Second Quarter	First Six Months
1. Maintain efficiency in the work force to a level of	97%	97.2%	98%	97.6%
2. Operate to a quality index of	70	82	89	85
3. Control perishable tools per man-hour worked so cost does not exceed	18¢ per man-hour	18¢	17.5¢	17.75¢
4. Control scrap percentage of the direct labor dollars earned so it does not exceed	.095%	.08%	.07%	.075%
5. Control factory supplied per man-hour worked so cost does not exceed	9¢ per man-hour	8.5¢	8¢	8.25¢
6. Maintain variables as budgeted:				
First quarter	$43,153	$45,477		
Second quarter	$35,820		$28,480	
First six months	$78,973			$73,957
7. Control unscheduled overtime so as not to exceed	$84.00 per week	$87.50	$86.50	$87.00
8. Control lost hours so as not to exceed	$325.00	$245.00	$105.00	$175.00
9. Maintain safety standards to the extent of no lost-time accidents and a reasonable amount of medicals		11 medicals, no lost time	10 medicals, no lost time	21 medicals, no lost time
10. Maintain housekeeping at the level of	100%	99%	99.5%	99.25%
11. Attain a cost-reduction goal of	$55,301	$12,508 (26% attained)	$62,490 (113% attained)	$74,998 (139% attained)

Key Result Areas	Measurement Factors (What to Measure)	Standards of Performance	Basis of Measurement (How to Measure)
Production	a. Quantity	a. Ninety percent of plant work capacity to be available excluding contract power interruptions.	a. Production Records
	b. Quality	b. Max. of 4 valid complaints/yr. for liquid NaOh, Cl_2, liquid KOH, H_2, max. of 6 complaints for Anhydrous Caustic.	b. Complaint Records
	c. Costs	c. Maintain production costs at 1968 standards level.	c. Cost Sheet
Maintenance	a. Costs	a. Maintain repair costs at 1967 standards level.	a. Cost Records
	b. Plant condition	b. Maintain plant at 1967 level—overall condition	b. Judgment
Personnel Relations	a. Safety	a. (1) Maintain average Hg vapor concentration in Cell Room at a/cu.m. or less. (2) Maintain accident frequency rate at 3.14 disabling injuries/million man hrs. worked or less.	a. (1) Vapor Records (2) Safety Records
	b. Employment and Turnover	b. (1) Keep hourly turnover below 2%. (2) Increase minority employment by 2% by 8/1/69.	b. (1) Personnel Report (2) EEO Report
Manpower Development	a. Quality	a. (1) One man ready to promote to 4-level by 9-15. One man ready to move to 3-level by 9-15. (2) Add two persons to IDP list by 10-1.	a. (1) Judgment (2) IDP Record
Public Relations	a. Community Relations	a. At least 4 speeches/yr. to civic and community groups.	a. Speech Record
	b. Plant Tours	b. At least 3 tours/yr. for civic, school groups, etc.	b. Tour Record
	c. Pollution Work	c. Serve actively on Pollution Control Board.	c. Judgment
Inventory Control	a. Investment in Stores Inventory	Maintain an adequate inventory based on maximums and minimums established by Plant Operating & Maintenance personnel.	Inventory Reports
Supervision	a. Productivity	Provide prompt service on issues—holding waiting time to a minimum. Receive, inspect and place material within 48 hours.	Complaints Records

Key Result Areas	Measurement Factors (What to Measure)	Standards of Performance	Basis of Measurement (How to Measure)
	b. Morale	Maintain good morale and teamwork in Department.	Judgment Personnel Reports
	c. Housekeeping	Maintain a safe, neat, efficient Stores Dept.	Appearance
Low Value and Blanket Order Releases	a. Orderliness	Procure items as required within limits as set forth by Office Manager and S.P.I.	Records—Releases
Surplus and Salvage Program	a. Cost Reduction	Prepare lists in conjunction with Maintenance and Operating personnel.	Judgment
Stores Records	a. Efficient Operation	Maintain accurate current records as required.	Judgment Records

Manager, Tech & Production

Key Result Areas	Measurement Factors (What to Measure)	Standards of Performance	Basis of Measurement (How to Measure)
Production Management	a. Cost	Total of positive volume and mfg. variance in combined resin plants. Bayonne positive by $12,500. Attain budget on paste resin start-up at Delaware City.	Production Cost Reports
	b. Quality	Suspension O.G.—Low Designator Paste Resin O.G.—Low Designator Copolymer O.G. Maximum no. of quality complaints (excl. Bayonne)	Sales and Plant Summary Reports
	c. Meeting production and shipping schedules	14 failures per year—Delaware City and Deer Park	Sales Reports
New Product and Process Development	a. No. of new products and processes	5 per year	E&D Status Reports
	b.	70% of projects within budgeted time plus 2 months	E&D Status Reports
	c. Increased sales attributable to new products	10% of sales dollars on products introduced both this and prior two years	Sales Reports
	d. Meet projected production cost	Meet each project reasonably.	E&D Status Reports and Plant Product Costs

Key Result Areas	Measurement Factors (What to Measure)	Standards of Performance	Basis of Measurement (How to Measure)
	e. Reduced production costs from new processes	7 significant cost saving innovations from all plants including Bayonne	Special Reports Monthly Plant Production Costs
New Applications Development	a. Number of projects	4 successful key projects per year and progress on continuing projects	SAL Progress Reports
	b. Meet timetable per project	70% of significant projects to be completed within time plus two months	SAL Progress Reports
	c. Increased sales attributable to applications projects	10% of sales dollar via new applications	Sales Reports
Provide Technical Service	a. Quality of work	Subjective	Sales Reports and
	b. Meet estimated cost per TSMR	Net of 15% over budget limits— $50 to $500, 10% over $500	Project Cost Report
	c. Timeliness	Net of 15% overdue on budgeted time and one week	Y/S Status Report
Develop and Maintain Effective Organization	a. Personnel turnover		Quarterly Y/O
	b. Trained manpower reserve	Subjective	Quarterly Y/O
	c. Personnel efficiency	Subjective	Quarterly Y/O
	d. Morale	Subjective	
Control of Costs	a. Production costs	See 1-a.	
	b. E&D costs	Budget ± 5%	E&D Cost Report
	c. Direct tech service costs	Average cost per TSMR of $325	Project Cost Report
	d. Applications lab costs	Budget ± 5%	Applications Cost
	e. Service costs other than above	Budget ± 10%	P&E Report
Planning and Analysis	a. Assure adequate facilities, materials and manpower	Able to meet sales demands on schedule	Subjective
	b. Seek,	3 important new ideas in Technical and Production per year, one of which is a personal idea	SAL, H&D, S&E Plant Reports

Key Result Areas	Measurement Factors (What to Measure)	Standards of Performance	Basis of Measurement (How to Measure)
	c. Cost foremost of products, processes and facilities	(1) Pro (2) Subjective on non-appropriations	Special, H&D
Respond to and Advise Division Management	a. Promptness		
	b. Clarity	Subjective	
	c. Value Or No., Clarity, and value of suggestions—some of high value		

Goals for Financial Managers

Senior Vice President—Finance*

Financial Planning

Satisfactory performance in financial planning has been attained when:

1. A complete three-year financial plan, including forecasts of all internal sources of funds and all requirements for funds, is prepared annually and revised, if necessary, at least twice during the year.

2. Recommendations are submitted to the President for new financing to provide any external funds required by the financial plan.

3. Open-market purchases of senior securities in anticipation of sinking-fund requirements are made at advantageous prices when possible and when funds for such purchases are available and authorized for such use.

4. Funds to cover all expenditures anticipated in the financial plan are immediately available for payments when required, from cash balances, liquidation of short-term investments, or new financing, without undue penalties from loss of interest income, premium penalties or other factors.

5. The capital structure of the company is maintained on a basis which does not restrict the choice of method of new financing when required.

*Reprinted by permission of the publisher, from *Objectives and Standards of Performance in Financial Management,* AMA Research Study #87, by Ernest C. Miller, pp. 74–76 © 1968 American Management Association, New York. All rights reserved.

6. The indirect obligations of the company through guarantees, long-term leases, and similar indirect pledges of credit do not adversely affect its long-term direct credit.

7. Excess funds not currently required to maintain minimum bank balances are invested in short-term securities which, on an annual basis, provide a greater average rate of return than that available from short-term U.S. Treasury bills.

8. Working capital is adequate but not excessive; and the current ratio, measured monthly, is not less than _____ nor more than _____ to _____.

9. Total of cash and equivalent at the end of each month is more than _____% of the monthly average of sales and operating revenue for the preceding 12 months.

10. Bank credit available is at least twice the amount of bank debt outstanding, except when unplanned major transactions requiring immediate availability of substantial sums are concluded through bank borrowing. (This does not imply that such bank credit shall be supported by a definitive bank credit agreement, but it may be supported by lines of credit or other indications of availability.)

11. Senior long-term debt carries an investment rating of A or better by Moody's Investors Service and Standard & Poor's.

Investor Relations

Satisfactory performance in investor relations has been attained when:

1. Investment analysts, representing institutional investors and investment advisors, regularly visit the company's offices to review its operations and outlook.

2. Presentations summarizing the company's operations and outlook are made at appropriate intervals to organized groups of security analysts.

3. Sound and friendly relationships are maintained with the financial press.

Investment Management

Satisfactory performance in investment management has been attained when:

1. At least three meetings are held each year with representatives of the trustee of the Retirement Plan Trust Fund to review investment performance of the trust fund and investment policy.

2. Periodic communication is maintained with the trustee of the Retirement Plan Trust Fund, between the aforesaid meetings, with respect to investment policy and specific investment transactions.

3. A flow of investment intelligence from security analysts is maintained to provide source material on general investment market trends and specific investments for assistance in the discussions of investment policy and investments with trustee.

4. A report is presented to the Board of Directors annually on the investment portfolio and investment performance of the Retirement Plan Trust Fund.

Insurance

Satisfactory performance in insurance of the operations and properties of the company has been attained when:

1. All properties, other than those self-insured, are covered by insurance at replacement values approved by department heads responsible for such properties.

2. Insurance against public liability and property damage to others is carried in a total amount approved periodically by the President.

3. Insurance costs giving consideration to claims collected are regularly compared with requested proposals from others and are found to be competitive.

4. Claims against the company are expeditiously settled when public relations or business relations are important factors.

Organization and Management Development

Satisfactory performance in organization and management development has been attained when:

1. The functions and responsibilities delegated by the President are allocated to positions which are described and coordinated in organization charts, position descriptions, and management guides which are kept currently up to date.

2. Authority and responsibility are appropriately delegated to the positions where decisions can be made most competently, and such delegations are expressed in writing.

3. Each manager who reports to the Senior Vice-President has standards of performance which have been approved by the Senior Vice-President.

4. Management positions are filled by individuals with the experience and knowledge required, and current or potential replacements have been identified for such positions.

   There is evidence that at least two candidates whose qualifications for promotion or transfer have been established prior to the time a vacancy occurs have been identified for each managerial position one and two levels below the Senior Vice-President—Finance. This includes all men who report to the Senior Vice-President—Finance and all managers who report to those men. (For this purpose, one person can be a candidate for several jobs.)

a. The qualifications of at least one of the candidates warrant his classification as ready now for the identified position.

b. At least one of the candidates represents a future replacement who is classified as ready after further development or experience.

c. Candidates from other departments are identified, to the extent practicable.

5. An annual review is made of the performance of each individual holding a management position, with counseling or corrective action when indicated.

Security of Information

Satisfactory performance has been attained with respect to safeguarding corporate information when there is in effect, for the Senior Vice-President's staff and for the function of each manager reporting to him, a written statement of procedure for implementing the company policy on security of corporate information as it applies to such staff and functions and when the company is not adversely affected by the disclosure of information under conditions contrary to such policy.

Specific Objectives

Satisfactory performance on specific subjects for any year has been attained when:

1. Objectives scheduled for accomplishment within the year are completed or attained as scheduled; or in the event a change in schedule or a change in external conditions beyond control has delayed completion or attainment, a satisfactory explanation of the reasons for such change is presented.

2. Progress is made on objectives scheduled for accomplishment in a future year, either in accordance with a schedule previously established or in a degree which indicates ultimate attainment by the target date.

3. A report on accomplishment of specific objectives for any year is submitted to the President with reasonable promptness after the close of such year.

Division Accountant

Key Result Areas	Measurement Factors (What to Measure)	Standards of Performance	Basis of Measurement (How to Measure)
Preparation and Analysis of Financial, Accounting and Statistical Reports	a. Promptness	Meet all deadlines	(F) Deadline Check-Off Control
	b. Accuracy	No major errors	(F) No. major errors made
	c. Effectiveness & significance	Provide information sought in understandable manner	(J) & (F) Min. of Questions
Recommend, Indicate and/or Conduct Special Projects & Studies of Accounting, Analytical and Procedural Nature	a. Satisfactory Completion of studies & projects	By specified due date a. Provide information sought in understandable manner	(F) Deadline Check-Off Control
	b. Effectiveness & significance	b. Of value sufficient to enable decision to be made	(J) & (F) Min. of Questions
Preparation of Budget and Profit Plan	a. Coordination	a. Sufficient to meet all interim deadlines b. Satisfactory planning	(F) Deadline Check-Off List
	b. Promptness	Meet all deadlines	(J) By Adm. Asst.
	c. Accuracy	No major errors	No. of errors made
	d. Analysis	Clear and understandable	Min. of Questions

Source: Diamond Shamrock, Dallas, Texas.

Accountant

Key Result Areas	Measurement Factors (What to Measure)	Standards of Performance	Basis of Measurement (How to Measure)
Accounting	a. Cost Reporting	Prepare all cost records as required by Cleveland Monthly, Quarterly and Annual.	Records
	b. Budget	Prepare Budgets in conjunction with Operating and Maintenance personnel.	Records, S.P.I.
	c. Cost Control	Prepare reports necessary by Industrial Chem. Plant to assist them in cost reduction.	Reports, Cost Reductions
Payroll	a. Preparation	Supervise preparation of payroll to assure accurate payment to employees.	Complaints
	b. Reports	Supervise and assure accurate reports as required by S.P.I.	Reports
Personnel	a. Morale	Supervise personnel to gain flexibility, teamwork in department. Accomplish work with minimum of overtime.	Personnel Records, Complaints

Source: Diamond Shamrock, Dallas, Texas.

Goals for Marketing and Sales Managers

Salesman

Key Result Areas	Measurement Factors (What to Measure)	Standards of Performance	Basis of Measurement (How to Measure)
Sales	a. Tons	± 5% of 19_____ budget in each product category	Quarterly Commodity Report
	b. Sales increase	Maintain at least av. increase for all salesmen in branch.	Monthly Report
Costs	a. Controllable Expense	Ratio expense/sales lower than 19_____	Quarterly Op. Statement
Accounts	a. No. of accounts	(1) 5 additional T/L consumers in 19_____, 30 additional T/L consumers in 19_____	(1) Monthly Reports (2) Monthly Reports
		(2) No. of new accts. added to be twice of accts. lost	
Reporting	a. Trade reports	Update each T/L or C/L user of our products—to identify market potential—by 7-1.	Reports to Mktg. Srs.
	b. Call reports	On all split credit accts., at least 1 report/qtr	Reports
Target Accounts	a. Tons—Dollars	(1) By 9-1, formally develop program for selling new or old Key accts. in territory using target accts. forms and submit to Branch Mgr	(1) Report to Branch Mgr.
		(2) Sell minimum of ½ new target accts. for 19_____	(2) Monthly Report
Personal Development	a. Conferences b. Communication	Attend min. of 1 program in one of following areas: modern marketing techniques, sales supervision, general management. Join and participate in Toastmasters Club.	Record of Attendance Record of Participation

Source: Diamond Shamrock, Dallas, Texas.

Sales Manager

Key Responsibilities (Key Result Areas)	Measurement Factors	Basis of Measurement (Source of Information)
Sales Pounds and Dollar Volume	a. Sales volume by product class	(F) Flash Report
	b. Sales price by product class	(F) Profit Analysis
	c. Share of market	(F) Tariff Comm. Rpt.
Control of Costs	a. Selling costs	(F) P&L
	b. Technical service costs	(F) P&L
	c. Distribution costs	(F) Dist. Cost Analysis
	d. Inventory size	(F) Profit Analysis
Development and Maintenance of Effective Organization	a. Personnel turnover	(F) T/O Analysis
	b. Trained manpower reserve	(F) T/O Analysis
	c. Personnel efficiency	(J) By G.M.
	d. Morale	(J) By G.M.
Market Planning and Analysis	a. End use participation	(1) (F) Tariff Comm. Report
		(2) (F) Tariff Comm. Report
		(3) (F) Flash Report
	b. Accuracy of forecasts	(F) Forecast Analysis
	c. Success of sales programs on new products	(F) Prod. Mgr. Report
	d. Contribution of new ideas to management and R&D—PVC and others	(J) By G.M.
Customer and Business Community Relations	a. Customer gain-loss	(F) Flash Report
	b. Service complaints	(F) Complaint Report Analysis
	c. Amount and type of publicity	(J) By G.M.
	d. Participation in business community activities	(J) By G.M.
Recommend and Advise in Division Management Decisions	a. Promptness	(J) By G.M.
	b. Clarity	(J) By G.M.
	c. Value	(J) By G.M.

Goals for a Variety of Other Staff Positions

General Counsel

Key Results Areas	Indicators	Objectives
Legal Advice to Other Departments	a. % of total items referred to outside counsel	a. To have no more than 10% referred to outside counsel by (date) with no increase in present department budget.
	b. Processing time	b. 1. To respond within 24 hours to all requests from Department heads or above by (date). 2. To respond within one week to requests of non-department heads by (date).
	c. Number of suits filed against the company after internal legal advice	c. To have no more than 10% of matters resulting in suit after following legal advice by (date).
Legal Documents, Minutes, Press Releases and Proxy Materials	a. % of total items referred to outside counsel	a. To have no more than 10% referred to outside counsel by (date) with no increase in department budget.
	b. Processing time	b. 1. To reduce drafting time of legal document and minutes to five days by (date). 2. To issue press releases within 24 hours date when info. is made available by (date). 3. To reduce routing time to two days by (date). 4. To have proxy material work schedule detailed & dovetailed before work begins by (date).
	c. Overtime work	c. To eliminate overtime work on proxy materials by (date).
	d. Complaints or disputes from within and outside company	d. To have no more than 10% of legal document drafted resulting in complaints or disputes.
Legal Conflicts (Litigation, Collection of Bad Debts, Policy Disputes & Contract Disputes)	a. Processing time	a. To process all department-level referrals within one week by (date).
	b. Items delegated	b. To have investment dept. preparing all collection letters by (date) at cost of 45 work-hours.
	c. Actual/predicted results	c. To anticipate and develop recommendations for 75% of variance in advance of monthly reviews with President.

Key Results Areas	Indicators	Objectives
	d. Disposition time	d. To have 90% of all litigation completed within one year by (date).
	e. Comments from those directly responsible for the area involved in conflict	e. To develop recommendations based on "Help & Hinders" survey of all department heads by (date).
Liaison with Government Agencies	a. Response time	a. To respond to all correspondence within five days by (date).
	b. Comments of agency personnel and staff	b. To develop recommendations based on "Helps and Hinders" survey of 2 highest priority agency directors.
Legal Department Administration	a. Number of scheduled completions missed	a. To miss no scheduled completions during remainder of year.
	b. Comments from legal staff	b. To develop objectives and action plans based on helps/hindrances survey of legal staff by (date).
	c. Need to repeat or clarify instructions	c. 1. To write Law Dept. Manual by (date). 2. To reduce repeats of instructions to less than 10% by (date).
Company Operations	a. Compliance of current company practices with laws and regulations	a. 1. To develop recommendations based on complete legal audit by (date). 2. To conduct complete legal audit annually thereafter.
	b. Participation in new projects	b. To participate in first stage development of all major new projects.
Relationships	a. Comments from superiors, department heads, and other personnel	a. To ask for comments on service once a quarter beginning by (date).
	b. Awareness by other departments of Legal Dept. workload	b. To distribute to all department heads anticipated workload of Legal Dept. by (date).
Personal Growth	a. Knowledge of accounting practices	a. To read (and identify at least two applications of) *Financial Reporting Practices of Corporations* by (date).
	b. Courses to be taken and applied	b. To complete Art of Negotiating Seminar and apply to one major project by (date).
	c. Reading	c. To read daily legal services within 24 hours by (date).
	d. Status of personal long-range plans	d. To develop life plan by (date).
	e. Personal health	e. 1. To reduce weight from 215 to 195 by (date). 2. To maintain weight of 195 for remainder of year.

Director of Employee & Public Relations

Key Result Areas	Measurement Factors	Performance
Administration of Division	a. Annual budget	Did Dept. function within 19_____ budget? Did I submit 19_____ budget by 11/15?
	b. Progress reports: written and oral	Turnover (quarterly), Personnel (monthly), Salary (periodically), Recruiting (annually), Labor (continually). Were they adequately interpreted for management's use?
	c. Plans for 19_____	These are the objectives outlined in Performance Review form.
	d. Does Dept. give better-than-average service to other units of company?	A continuing objective
	e. Is our research work such that we are keeping competitive as far as personnel programs and policies are concerned?	Continuing process. Reports on salary and pension surveys, wage and benefit surveys, Chlor-Alkali data, etcetera
	f. Do I develop members of Dept. in all-around efficiency; guide personnel in carrying out assigned responsibilities; build them towards assuming greater responsibilities?	*Continuing.* Do they get on-the-job training? Switch jobs without hurting efficiency? Do I *let* and *make* each supervisor present programs in *his* area to top management and not take over myself?
	g. Is our recruiting effort meeting company goals?	
External and Internal Relations	a. Attend the many meetings scheduled with top and middle management of Diamond.	Conduct myself with efficiency. Contribute where possible; listen where I cannot contribute.
	b. Image C.R.B. and Dept. have within Diamond.	Cooperative, effective; prompt, knowledgeable. Are we a positive factor in Diamond's success.
	c. What is C.R.B. and Emp. and Pub. Rel. Dept.'s reputation outside of Diamond?	Do we conduct A.M.A. sessions; give talks at schools, churches, personnel associations; attend M.C.A. Ind. Rel. Com. meetings, Chlor-Alkali meetings, etc.? Do we have many sessions with govt. officials on various matters?
Manpower Area		
1. Supply Qualified Manpower	a. Number of complaints	Minimum over the year
	b. Delay in filling jobs	Reasonable time
	c. College recruiting quota	Yearly report; percent of quota
2. Management Development	a. Has it been sold? Is it working? Are we doing good job educating in this area?	We should have forms on all people "promotable" by 3/1.
	b. Is it competitive?	Are we meeting standards of Management Development Program?

Key Result Areas	Measurement Factors	Performance
3. Performance Review	a. Does system measure performance and does it improve performance? Is it used?	Spot check a number of forms to see if objectives are met. Percent of forms turned in. Percent of people not receiving Performance Reviews.
4. Manpower Forecast	a. Are forms and procedures followed?	All should be in by 10/1/____.
	b. Accuracy of forecasts (actual vs. estimated)	At least 85% accuracy in first 2 years and 70% in next 3.
	c. Availability of manpower	Three out of 4 jobs filled with available manpower.
Labor Relations	a. Negotiating of Painesville pension	By 7/22/____, within competitors' formulas
	b. Advise and counsel on other labor contracts	Long-term contracts on dates of termination
	c. Advise, recommend changes in non-union plants designed to keep non-union status	
	d. Have we maintained non-union plants without paying more than union in wages and benefits?	
	e. Where elections were held, did we handle campaigns efficiently?	Not to lose because of lack of well-advised campaign
Employee Benefits	a. Do we have a competitive benefit program?	Survey of our competitors
	b. Do we get maximum value for minimum cost?	What percent of benefits' cost to sales?
	c. Job Evaluation Program—is it effective?	(1) Control reports (2) Use of job description
Public Relations	a. Diamond's image	Comments from financial community and other sources inside and outside company
	b. Internal and external communication	On time; accurate
	c. Publicity in press and magazines	What kind of coverage? How broad? How good?
General Personnel	a. Counsel and advise all employees on transfers, promotions, early retirements, departmental reorganization	
	Personal	

Source: Diamond Shamrock, Dallas, Texas.

Purchasing Agent

Key Result Areas	Measurement Factors	Performance
Buying	a. Price	Purchase material assigned to lowest cost consistent without quality required.
	b. Quality	Meet specifications with no justifiable complaints.
	c. Delivery	No significant interference with Production, Maintenance or Construction schedules resulting from late deliveries of materials or services.
	d. Services	All vendors furnish services as requested by plant supervisory personnel.
	e. Industrial Relations	Promote a good image of DACO in area by: purchasing materials and services locally whenever practical; be fair and honest in daily contacts with visitors and sales personnel.
	f. Plant Relations	Provide assistance to plant supervisors in obtaining necessary supplies and services for better plant operation.
Purchasing Research	a. Cost Reduction	Investigate and recommend new or substitute materials and new approaches that will result in lower cost plant operations.
		Improve the present sources of supply and develop new and better vendors for materials and services.
		Three innovations per year.
Supervisory Responsibilities	a. Morale	Maintain above average morale in the Dept.
	b. Salary Administration	Make each salary commensurate with the job and individual's performance.
	c. Productivity	Attempt to hold present level of personnel.
	d. Budget	Establish realistic Dept. budget which can be met within ± 5%.
Surplus Disposal	a. Cost Reduction	All materials declared surplus by plant supervisors and inventory analysis committee be disposed of promptly and in accordance with company policy and procedure.
Staff Functions	a. Plant Performance	Contribute practical suggestions that aid in solving plant problems.
	b. Public relations	Participate in local civic affairs.

Plant Office Manager

Key Result Areas	Measurement Factors	Performance
Office Services	a. Office Equipment	(1) Keep total cost of equipment usage *below* previous year's level.
		(2) No equipment downtime more than 1 day due to repairs.
	b. Budget	(1) Meet budget ± 5%.
		(2) Keep GWE % of cost at or below previous year's levels.
Accounting	a. Payroll	No more than 1 error/pay period
	b. Reports	No late reports to Division or Corporate
	c. Property	Account for property according to S.P.I. with zero deviations.
	d. Internal Audits	Assist public auditors and Corporate Audit Staff as requested with excellent cooperation.
Traffic	a. Billing	Report shipments to cusomters and Co. Traffic Dept.—same day—4 errors/yr. allowable.
	b. Tank Car-Truck	Quarterly tank car and truck control report to Cleveland by 3-15, 6-15, 9-15, 12-31, no errors
Personal Development	a. Reading	Read at least 1 book: for example, management, and report.
	b. Conference	Attend at least 1 program: Diamond conducted or outside company.

Source: Diamond Shamrock, Dallas, Texas.

Quiz

Goal-Driven Management in Different Situations:
A Collection of Approaches

1. Have you successfully used goal-driven management   _____ _____
    in the public sector: Yes   No

    Comments:

2. Have you successfully used goal-driven management   _____ _____
    in staff departments?   Yes   No

    Comments:

3. Have you successfully used goal-driven management   _____ _____
    in sales and marketing?   Yes   No

    Comments:

4. Have you successfully used goal-driven management   _____ _____
    in non-profit organizations?   Yes   No

    Comments:

5. Have you successfully used goal-driven management   _____ _____
    with blue collar workers?   Yes   No

    Comments:

Appendix B
Publications on the Application of Goal-Driven Management in Different Settings

Allen, Marisal G. *The Use of Management By Objectives with Classroom Teachers.* Ed.D. Dissertation, The University of Tennessee, 1972.

Deegan, Arthur X. *Management by Objectives for Hospitals.* Germantown, PA: Aspen Publications, 1977.

Deegan, Arthur X. and Roger Fritz. *MBO Goes to College.* Boulder, CO: Division of Continuing Education, Bureau of Independent Study, 1975.

Deegan, William L. and others. *Community College Management By Objectives.* Sacramento, CA: California Junior College Assn., 1974.

Grindley, Kit and Hymble, John W. *The Effective Computer: A Management by Objectives Approach.* New York: AMACOM, 1974.

Harvey, L. James. *Management By Objectives in Higher Education.* Washington, DC: McManis Associates, Inc., 1974.

Harvey, L. James. *Managing Colleges and Universities by Objectives.* Littleton, CO: Ireland Educational Corporation, 1976.

Ijiki, Y. *Management Goals and Accounting for Control.* Chicago: Rand McNally, 1965.

Margolis, Fredric H. *Training By Objectives—A Participant-Oriented Approach.* Washington, DC: Behavioral Science Center, Sterling Institute, 1970.

McBurney, William J., Jr. *Goal Setting and Planning at the District Sales Level.* New York: American Management Association, Inc., AMA Research Study 61, 1963.

McConkey, Dale D. *Financial Management By Objectives.* Englewood Cliffs, NJ: Prentice-Hall, 1976.

McConkey, Dale D. *Management By Objectives for Staff Managers.* New York: Vantage Press, 1972.

McConkey, Dale D. *MBO for Non-Profit Organizations.* AMACOM, 1975.

Miller, Ernest C. *Objectives and Standards of Performance in Financial Marketing.* New York: American Management Association, Research Study 87, 1968.

Miller, Ernest C. *Objectives and Standards: An Approach to Planning and Control.* New York: American Management Association, Research Study 74, 1966.

Miller, Ernest C. *Objectives and Standards of Performance in Marketing Management.* New York: American Management Association, Research Study 85, 1967.

Miller, Ernest C. *Objectives and Standards of Performance in Production Management.* New York: American Management Association, Research Study 84, 1967.

Norris, Graeme. *The Effective University: A Management by Objectives Approach.* Brookfield, VT: Renouf, USA, Inc., 1978.

Odiorne, George S. *Bank Management By Objectives.* American Bankers Association, 1970.

Odiorne, George S. *Personnel Administration by Objectives.* Homewood, IL: Richard D. Irwin, Inc., 1971.

Odiorne, George S. *Training by Objectives: An Economic Approach to Management Training.* New York: The Macmillan Company, 1970.

Odiorne, George S. and Hermanson, Roger H. *Programmed Learning Aid for Personnel Administration: A Management By Objectives Approach.* Homewood, IL: Richard D. Irwin, Inc., 1973.

Pascoe, B. J. *Case History of Management by Objectives Within the Civil Service.* Royal Navy Supply and Transport Service, Ministry of Defense (Navy), London, Great Britain, July, 1969.

Wiehe, Vernon R. *Management by Objectives in Mental Health Services.* Ann Arbor, MI: Masterco Press, Inc., 1974.

Appendix C
Who's Who in Management Today

The purpose of this list is to acknowledge some of the major contributors to the new approaches to management used in the U.S. today. It is not a complete list in any sense, nor is it a recommended list for those seeking consultation or advice. The selection of names was based upon the individual's contributions to the following: publishing, education, conference and workshop participation, and general support of new management ideas.

Individuals	Location
Abney, Bonnie	San Francisco, California
Albrecht, Karl G.	San Diego, California
Batton, J. D.	Des Moines, Iowa
Beck, Arthur	Richmond, Virginia
Blanchard, Kenneth	Amherst, Massachusetts
Coffee, Donn	New York City, New York
Drucker, Peter	Los Angeles, California
Handscombe, Richard S.	United Kingdom
Hillmar, Ellis D.	Richmond, Virginia
Hughes, Charles	Dallas, Texas
Humble, John W.	United Kingdom
Ivancevich, John M.	Houston, Texas
Kirchhoff, Bruce A.	Omaha, Nebraska
Kirkpatrick, Donald	Milwaukee, Wisconsin
Mahler, Walter R.	New York City, New York
Mali, Paul	Groton, Connecticut
McConkey, Dale D.	Madison, Wisconsin
Migliore, R. Henry	Tulsa, Oklahoma
Miller, Ernest	New York City, New York
Morrisey, George L.	Los Angeles, California
Odiorne, George	Amherst, Massachusetts
Ouchi, William	Los Angeles, California
Patton, Thomas H.	Lansing, Michigan

Peters, Thomas	Palo Alto, California
Raia, Anthony P.	Los Angeles, California
Reddin, A. J.	Bermuda
Seyna, Gene	Rochester, New York
Tosi, Henry L.	Lansing, Michigan
Varney, Glenn H.	Bowling Green, Ohio
Weihrich, Heinz	San Francisco, California
Waterman, Robert	San Francisco, California

Appendix D
Additional Reading on New
Management Ideas

This is a selected listing of material written on new management ideas intended to expand your awareness of new and proven approaches to effective management.

Books

Albrecht, Karl G. *Successful Management By Objectives—An Operational Approach.* Englewood Cliffs, NJ: Spectrum Book, 1977.

Blanchard, K. and Johnson, S. *The One Minute Manager.* New York: William Morrow & Company, 1982.

Deegan, Arthur X. *Management By Objectives for Hospitals.* Germantown, PA: Aspen Publications, 227 pages.

Fulmar, Robert M. and Theodore J. Herbert. *Exploring the New Management, A Study Guide with Cases, Readings, Incidents, and Exercises.* New York: Macmillan Publishing Co., Inc., London: Collier Macmillan Publishing, 2nd edition, 1978.

Heirs, B. and G. Pehrson. *The Mind of the Organization.* New York: Harper & Row Publishing, 1982.

Naisbitt, J. *Megatrends.* New York: Warner Books, 1982.

Norris, Graeme. *The Effective University: A Management By Objectives Approach.* Brookfield, VT: Renouf, USA, Inc., 1978.

Odiorne, George S. *The Encyclopedia of Professional Management,* L. Bitte, Chapter 5, "Management by Objectives—Update." New York: McGraw-Hill, 1977.

Odiorne, George S., H. Weciach, and J. Mendleson. *Executive Skills: An MBO Approach.* Dubuque: W. C. Brown, 1980.

Odiorne, George S. *MBO II, A System of Managerial Leadership.* Belmont, CA: Fearon·Pitman, 1979.

Odiorne, George S. Portuguese Translation: *Management Decisions By Objectives,* published by LTC, Av. Venezuelo 163, Rio de Janeiro, Brazil, 1977.

Ouchi, W. *Theory Z.* Reading, MA: Addison-Wesley Publishing, 1981.

Pascale, T., and A. Athos. *The Art of Japanese Management.* New York: Warner Books, 1981.

Peters, T. J., and R. H. Waterman. *In Search of Excellence.* New York: Harper & Row Publishing, 1982.
Smith, H. R., Archer Carroll, Asterios G. Kefalas, Hugh J. Watson. *Management, Making Organizations Perform.* New York: Macmillan Publishing Co., 1980.

Articles

Abdelsamad, Moustafa H. "Financial Management of Small Business in Difficult Times," *Management World,* Vol. 9, No. 1, January, 1980, pp. 26–28.
Lewis, M. "Management By Objectives—Review, Application, and Relationship with Job Satisfaction and Performance," *Journal of Academic Librarianship,* Vol. 5, No. 6, 1980, pp. 329–334.
McConkey, Dale D. "Building Toward MBO," *Data Management,* Vol. 18, No. 1, January, 1980, pp. 44–47.
Shipper, Frank M. "Anticipatory Management—The Key to the Eighties," *Management World,* Vol. 9, No. 1, January, 1980, pp. 15–16, 28.
Werner, Frank. "Commercial Software," *Computerworld,* Vol. 14, No. 1, December 31–January 7, 1980, pp. 17–22.

Index

About the Author

Glenn H. Varney, Ph.D., is professor of management and director of the Master in Organization Development program at Bowling Green State University. He is also president of MAA Inc., a consulting firm in human resource and organization development. He has had three books published, with two more in press on team building and the change process. He has also published more than fifty articles in a variety of professional journals. Dr. Varney was director of the OD Division and Vice-President of A.S.T.D. He holds several awards, including the A.S.T.D. Torch Award. He earned his Ph.D. at Case Western Reserve University.